HELLO AGAIN!

In the five years since we published *Differences That Make a Difference*, leaders across the globe in public and private sectors serving organizations of all sizes, have made significant strides in harnessing the power that derives from a workplace where differences are front and center. If you have read our book, you will remember that we moved from the concept of "diversity" to one of "inclusion." That decision was and remains far more than semantics; indeed, it is a recognition that when diversity, however it is articulated, is considered the end game, the tournament is lost. There may indeed be no more games played unless the next vital step—inclusion—arrives in time.

For the last couple of years, COVID plodded and then rumbled across one country after another, where leaders faltered, death and destruction followed. Then the Russian advance in Ukraine erupted. We are now facing some economic headwinds and shifting workforce trends. As if that was not enough, we have had a severe supply-chain problem that has impacted most industries; and in the name of national security, we have new and vast trade restrictions with China that are impacting the technology industries anywhere from mildly to severely. So, as a people, we have been dealing with one unwelcome drama after another, and the consensus seems to be that what we once called "normal" has no path on which to return. Effective leadership has perhaps never been more crucial. Alvin Toffler, the author of the book *Future Shock*, published years ago when we believed we were smugly, "in control," phrased it well: "The illiterate of the 21st century will not be those who cannot read and write, but those who cannot learn, unlearn and relearn." Here, again, there is a crucial next step: what will we do with all that we relearn?

This book is less a sequel to our earlier work than it is a refinement and expansion of those ideas. And we have tried to enhance and improve what we provide you, our reader. These additions are in themselves the product of paying close attention to the need to "practice what we preach." Here are three significant examples:

1. There is every reason to believe that we can extend that pulpit metaphor to the assumption that we are "preaching to the choir." If you are reading this book—and at least so far you are—the chances are excellent that you either see yourself as a leader or have every intention of becoming one.

   Arguably, then, we should focus on macro-trends, leadership skills, and catchy alliterative phrases such as "the courage to change." And we will, but we will add data and skill-building tips addressed to those who, no matter what their position in a community or company, have not merely witnessed, but felt the welcome effects of inclusion and might also continue to contend with the scars from its absence.

2. There is no question that one can find in bookstores and libraries—along with perhaps some public restrooms—books and magazine articles on inclusion and its cousins: diversity and equality. A substantial majority of these deal with large-scale enterprises. In this book, we hope to both recognize the needs and pass along the experiences of small and mid-sized organizations as well. Whether you operate a single-owner-no-staff-yet LLC or occupy the corner office of the C-Suite in a multinational billions-plus corporation, we strive to provide you with something useful enough that you will pass it along to a friend or colleague before a week goes by. And throughout, we are choosing to add to what we have researched and reported on these pages. Ideas—speculations really-that may be yet unsupported with

Pedro is a distinguished thought leader on inclusion and the future of work. With the help of his co-authors, Jorge and Maria, Pedro has written an outstanding book on the return on inclusion. Don't miss out on this ROI. Definitely a must-read for the AI age.

ROCÍO PÉREZ | Creator of The MindShift Game

Pedro's journey exemplifies the power of action and perseverance in making a difference. Through his genuine connection with people and advocacy efforts, he has emerged as a globally recognized inclusion advocate. In this work, Pedro and his co-authors employ analogies and examples to foster awareness and promote genuine learning about the nuanced concept of inclusion.

LINDA HADDAD | Banking Leader and Startup Founder

The Real ROI delivers practical advice on creating inclusive teams and opening ourselves up to belonging by sharing wise insights from 50 top world leaders.

SHELLYE ARCHAMBEAU | Board Member of Verizon

The Real ROI on inclusion offers an unusual 360 view on the meaning and impact of inclusion. As the founder of a healthcare company operating in Bangladesh, one of the world's fastest growing economies, I learned so much. At this critical juncture in our global economy, leaders everywhere must reflect on how to embed inclusivity in our organizations.

SYLVANA QUADER SINHA | Founder, Chair, & CEO of Praava Health

This book is a page turner with wisdom from the authors' vast network on every page. This book is full of positivity and practicality, packed with thoughts and advice on how to advance inclusivity.

SHERYL H. EHRMAN | PhD, PE, Dean of the College of Engineering at San José State University

Pedro is an all-embracing multicultural leader. His entrepreneur experience and genuine connection with people from around the world, shines throughout *The Real ROI: Return On Inclusion*.

A must read towards addressing biases in the workplace—provides an equitable and respectful awareness in making people from diverse backgrounds included and engaged. It makes Inclusion easy to measure, and much easier to manage than diversity.

NANCY ESCOTO | ViceChair of PanPeru USA, Global Human Resources Executive, Gender Equality Advocate, WIN Executive Partner

The *Real ROI* offers a fresh perspective on inclusion in the AI sector. 2024 marks a year of substantial innovation and transformation. Pedro excels in compiling essential advice from 50 leading CEOs on embracing cultural intelligence to foster an inclusive workplace. As an eloquent keynote speaker and my mentee since his time at UC Berkeley at age 19, Pedro's insights are invaluable. I highly recommend this book.

JASON MA | CEO & Chief Mentor of ThreeEQ, Author of *Young Leaders 3.0* data because we believe strongly that innovation, defined by timing as much as it is by content, is key to a positive response in today's world. Climate change, for instance, is just one of many challenges that require transformative and perhaps even radical action now.

3. Research for a book like this one proves that other researchers and authors are calling on sources produced by a core of professional, articulate, and innovative writers in the business world. We do as well, but we purposefully have added sources and ideas from a broader base—philosophers, humorists, commentators, you name it.

Briefly put, we've plowed the ground and planted the fruit. You, as a reader, get to fill your plate.

In the fields of opportunity,
it's plowing time again.

~ Neil Young

THE REAL ROI: RETURN ON INCLUSION

Pedro David Espinoza
Maria Lensing
Jorge Titinger

ISBN: 979-8-218-43888-3

I dedicate this book to my mother Julia and father Pedro for always teaching me to work wholeheartedly for a higher purpose, for something greater. I am truly grateful and blessed because of both of you. This is for you mom and dad! In Christ,

Pedro David Espinoza

TABLE OF CONTENTS

ABOUT THE FOREWORD WRITER

CARLOS MIGUEL GUTIERREZ'S journey from a young immigrant fleeing Cuba to becoming a significant figure in American business and politics exemplifies a remarkable story of resilience and achievement. Born into a family affected by the Cuban Revolution's expropriations, Gutierrez's early life was marked by upheaval and relocation, first to the United States and then Mexico, before eventually settling in the U.S. again. Despite not completing his degree, his entry into the Kellogg Company marked the beginning of an illustrious career that saw him rise to become the CEO and later, the U.S. Secretary of Commerce.

Gutierrez's tenure at Kellogg was particularly transformative, with his "Volume to Value" strategy revitalizing the company amidst declining cereal sales. His approach, focusing on higher-margin products and robust marketing, not only turned around Kellogg's fortunes but also positioned him as a respected business leader, recognized by Fortune Magazine as "The Man Who Fixed Kellogg."

His transition to public service as the Secretary of Commerce under President George W. Bush further demonstrated his versatility and commitment to public service, playing pivotal roles in U.S.-Cuba policy, immigration legislation, and trade agreements. Gutierrez's advocacy for comprehensive immigration reform and economic policies, along with his involvement in trade agreements like CAFTA-DR, underscore his belief in the power of policy to drive economic growth and societal progress.

Post-administration, Gutierrez continued to engage in influential roles across the private sector and academia, contributing his expertise to various boards and think tanks. He served on the board of directors of Occidental Petroleum, MetLife, PwC (Price Water House Coopers), boards for University of Miami, The Woodrow Wilson International Center for Scholars (WWICS), Meridian

International Center, and Time Warner. His endorsements of Hillary Clinton and Joe Biden reflect his ongoing engagement with key political and social issues, emphasizing his commitment to pragmatic and inclusive policies.

Carlos Gutierrez's story is a testament to the potential for immigrants to profoundly impact their adopted countries, contributing to both the economic landscape and the broader societal fabric. His career spans significant achievements in both the corporate world and public service, highlighting the importance of adaptability, vision, and a commitment to contributing positively to society.

ABOUT THE AUTHORS

PEDRO DAVID ESPINOZA is a TED speaker, entrepreneur, AI investor, and author. In 2014, Pedro became the Founder & CEO of SmileyGo, an app that helped companies invest smarter. SmileyGo indexed the data of 1.3 million NGOs in addition to having users in 30 countries. Incubated at SkyDeck, his software startup gained funding from 1517 Fund, Frank Baxter, Jack Larson, and Berkeley Haas Seed Fund. In 2017, Janet Napolitano awarded Pedro The University of California Entrepreneur Winner. In 2018, Pedro founded Pan Peru USA, a venture that empowers women to become entrepreneurs. With the support from Fortune 500s, Pan Peru has scaled from empowering 1 to 100 women. In 2019, Pedro wrote a book with Jorge Titinger with contributions from Eric Schmidt, Reed Hastings, and Dan Schulman. Pedro's book—*Differences That Make a Difference*—attracted 100 CEOs as contributors such as Pat Gelsinger who wrote the foreword. His book received the 2020 Best Business Book Award by Latino International.

Educated at Berkeley, Stanford, and Harvard, Pedro began his career as a mechanic during his adolescence. In 2010, Pedro launched his music singles on Apple, Spotify and Amazon. Pedro is the Founder & General Partner of PDE Ventures, a venture capital fund that has twenty startup investments such as KiwiBot, Mocafi and Happioh. He is also a limited partner at venture capital funds such as Cortado Ventures, GoodLight Capital, and 1Flourish Capital. In 2021, *The Silicon Valley Business Journal* recognized him as a Latin Business Leadership Honoree.

In 2016, Pedro became a distinguished keynote speaker. Microsoft, Alphabet, and Meta are some of the companies he has given speeches. Pedro has given 300 keynotes on grit by sharing his entrepreneurial immigrant story. In 2020, he became an engineering lecturer at Tecnologico de Monterrey. In 2021, Pedro became a Special Advisor to Blue Shield's Chief Medical Officer

Dr. James Cruz. In 2024, Pedro's second book—*The Real ROI: Return on Inclusion*—attracted 50 CEOs as writing contributors such as Michael Dell, John Hennessy, and Shellye Archambeau.

Pedro has been profiled in *Forbes*, Nasdaq, Yahoo Finance, CBS, Univision, GlobeNewswire, Telemundo, Hispanic Shark Tank, *Times of Israel*, KRON-TV, Hispanic Executive, Latin America Reports, Al Día News, and *Latino Leaders Magazine*. In 2017, *The Voice of America* named Pedro "The Robinhood of Technology". Pedro serves on the board of directors of Melzi Surgical, Notre Dame de Namur University, Silicon Valley Tech Academy, ActAware, Loyal Card, Institute for International Medicine, Inkas Rent A Car, Autoespar, Lunahuana River Resort, and GESA.

In 2017, Pedro gave his TED Talk—Build the Bridge—sharing his American Dream story having 22,000 views. In 2020, Pedro joined the Silicon Valley Leadership Group as the VP of Business Development. In 2021, Pedro was elected as the Vice Curator for Global Shapers in Palo Alto by the World Economic Forum. In 2022, Pedro got accepted to the LinkedIn Creator Accelerator Program as a Technology & Innovation Awardee having 21,600 followers. Later, he became the CMO of Ever Medical Technologies to lead the marketing team. In 2023, Pedro received the NextGen 30 Under 30 Award presented by Goldman Sachs. Later, Pedro was appointed to the Advisory Board of 1t.org of the World Economic Forum. In 2024, Pedro received the Silicon Valley 40 Under 40 Award presented by BMO. Pedro's Pan Peru has given 3,000 children access to STEM education and reforested 15,000 trees. Pedro has received recognition for his success, he has received the 2021–2022 and 2022–2023 HITEC 100 Awards—which features the 100 most influential Latinos.

MARIA LENSING is responsible for the strategic technology plan to accelerate the long-term growth potential for Walgreens. She leads the development and execution of a consistent, strategic and transparent approach to how the technology organization delivers value to the business, as well as having responsibility for workforce strategy, strategic vendor management, supplier diversity, technology governance and compliance and financial management.

Prior to her current role, Maria was the Chief Technology Officer at McKesson, where she was responsible for developing McKesson's technology stack vision, strategy and architectures. She was critical to the acceleration of technology solutions to support vaccine distribution in the United States, earning the award of "CTO of the Year" by Tech Titans in 2021. Maria also delivered structural and operational improvements resulting in a 20% decline in business disruption in her first year in the role. She led McKesson through a transformational program to outsource technology operations that allowed a shift of resourcing and tech expertise towards business enablement.

Before that, Maria spent eleven years at AT&T in both technical and business leadership roles. She was VP of Healthcare Solutions at AT&T leading the full P&L responsibility for the $6B group. She led her team through the pandemic, playing a critical role in the COVID-19 Alliance, which delivered critical infrastructure acceleration and connectivity solutions to healthcare entities addressing the pandemic. She also brought the first 5G trials in healthcare to the United States, where the partnership with Vitas Healthcare and AR/VR solution delivered a 20% decrease in pain for hospice patients. Maria helped AT&T's largest healthcare customers reduce costly inefficiencies, maximize system availability and improve security and compliance while accelerating digital transformation for extraordinary business outcomes.

She was also Chief of Staff for the Chief Executive Officer of AT&T Business. As a member of the Executive Leadership Team,

Maria led business strategy and planning across the company, provided market insights to support investment and technology strategies, and informed the CEO agenda. Maria worked across the executive leadership team to develop the five-pillar strategy that defined business priorities and established the cadence for the management of the entire business. This led to reshaping the BU strategic business planning process in support of our business transformation, delivering sequential quarterly growth turning around the group's profitability one year faster than anticipated.

Maria has a Bachelor's of Science in Electrical Engineering and Master's of Science in Engineering Management from Christian Brothers University (CBU). She completed her Executive Education at Harvard Business School. She is an independent director at Sorenson Communications and a board director for the Hispanic IT Executive Council (HITEC). Maria is a boardroom certified Qualified Technology Expert (QTE).

Maria is passionate about STEM opportunities for youth, women in leadership and promoting minority inclusion in the executive ranks. She has received a lot of recognition, including the 2023 Top 100 Latinas by *Latino Leaders Magazine*. She was HITEC 100 leaders for 2022, 2021 and 2020. She was 2021 Corporate CTO of the year by Tech Titans of North Texas and 2019 Women in Business by the *Dallas Business Journal*. Maria is fluent in English and Spanish and has been published by the *Huffington Post*.

Maria and Brad, her husband, reside in Dallas, Texas with their two boys.

JORGE LUIS TITINGER is the founder and CEO of Titinger Consulting, a boutique consulting firm focused on strategy development, the cultural aspects of M&A, corporate transformations and leadership coaching. He is also the award-winning co-author (with Pedro Espinoza) of the book *Differences That Make a Difference* where he brings the thoughts and insights of over 100 top executives on the topic of inclusion and diversity, and its impact on the success of companies. Mr. Titinger has over thirty years of experience in the high tech industry and has held numerous executive and Board positions in the semiconductor equipment and computer industries. He is a sought after public speaker and advisor, his clients range from multi-billion dollar companies to start-ups.

Mr. Titinger served as the President, CEO and Director of Silicon Graphics (SGI), one of the leading global companies in high performance computing. Prior to SGI, Mr. Titinger served as President, CEO and Director of Verigy Inc., both companies were successfully turned-around and sold with excellent results for all stakeholders. Jorge held executive positions at Form Factor, KLA-Tencor, Applied Materials, Inc., and Hewlett-Packard. He is very involved in the start-up community both in the US and Peru; he is a mentor with Endeavor, and an LP in several venture funds.

Mr. Titinger has been named "CEO of the Year" in the Operational Effectiveness Category, by CEO World Awards in 2013, and was selected as one of the "Top 100 Latinos in Technology," by HITEC, in 2013, 2014, 2015, 2016 and 2018, and in 2017, was awarded the "Estrella Award" as the top Latino in Tech. Jorge is an LXCouncil Certified License Partner; he moderates a CEO—Peer to Peer Group where he leads a group of CEOs from different industries in their journey to maximize their success, working as a board of advisors in a confidential and trustworthy setting. He was selected as one of the top 10 Best of the Boardroom by *Hispanic Executive Magazine*. Most recently, he had been recognized by NACD as an honoree of the 2023 NACD Directorship 100™.

He has served and serves in multiple public, private, and non-profit Boards, including the public company Boards of Axcelis Technologies where he is currently Lead Director and the Chair of the Compensation Committee, CalAmp Corporation where he is currently the Chair of the Compensation Committee, Ichor Holdings and FormFactor, Inc. Mr. Titinger also served as a director of Xcerra Corporation from October 2012 until its acquisition in 2018 by Cohu, Inc., where he continued to serve as a director until May 2021. He is also on the Boards of the Hispanic Foundation of Silicon Valley, the Stanford Children's Hospital, the Education Foundation of Silicon Valley, Innovate Public Schools and Panasas. He holds a B.S. in Electrical Engineering, an M.S. in Electrical Engineering, and an M.S. in Engineering Management and Business, all from Stanford University.

Mr. Titinger was an accomplished athlete in his youth, he was the captain of the Stanford Varsity soccer team, and the captain of the USA national indoor soccer team from 1988 to 1993. He is passionate about education and improving the life of Latinos in the USA.

PAN PERU NONPROFIT ORGANIZATION

Given our backgrounds in entrepreneurship, business and technology, we believe that education is the best way to develop a community. Thus, we decided to support Pan Peru (www.panperu.org)—a 501(c)(3) nonprofit organization that builds libraries, computer labs, and greenhouses to empower the under-served youth of our Incan country.

We encourage you to support this charity as a fine way to educate economically disadvantaged children and women in Peru. Pan Peru has built ten libraries, nine greenhouses, and four computer labs, benefiting 3,000 children in the most remote places of our Andean nation.

Equally important, Pan Peru launched Alpaca Pan Peru (www.alpacapanperu.com) with the mission to empower women to become entrepreneurs. This program is helping seventy women (single mothers, divorced, or teenagers) become businesswomen by training them on how to design, produce, and market their handmade alpaca beanies, scarves, and sweaters.

You can support Pan Peru in three ways:
PayPal: www.paypal.me/panperuusa
Web: *www.panperu.org/web/donar-3/*
https://alpacapanperu.com/donate

Thank you,

Pedro, Maria, and Jorge

FOREWORD By Carlos Gutierrez (former CEO of Kellogg's, U.S. Secretary of Commerce)

Pedro Espinoza, Jorge Titinger and Maria Lensing are shrewd observers of societal and business trends. Their insights on diversity and inclusion are fresh with new perspectives; they take the discussion to a new level. This book is required reading for anyone interested in building high performing organizations. *The Real ROI* will improve leaders' behaviors in today's diverse organizations.

The Real ROI is the sequel to *Differences That Make a Difference* by Pedro Espinoza and Jorge Titinger. Their initial intent was to update the progress made with regards to DEI in the few years post the publication of their book. They were not counting on a pandemic, on the great resignation, on a supply chain crisis...so it is unclear whether there had been any "progress" or whether the issue had just morphed into something else. So they joined forces with Maria Teresa Lensing, and in practicing what they preached, brought diversity of thought and experience to the creation of *The Real ROI.*

In the realm of progress and change, their journey never truly ended; it merely took new turns and forms. As we gather once again within the pages of this consequential sequel, we are reminded of the constant evolution of ideas and movements. The powerful resonance of *Differences That Make a Difference* remains relevant through time, and illuminates our path as we delve into its important continuation.

In the wake of the unprecedented challenges that the global pandemic thrust upon us, the course of the Diversity, Equity, and Inclusion (DEI) movement was forever altered. As we eagerly embark on the chapters of this follow-up, we find ourselves navigating uncharted territory, where the intersections of DEI and transformation have become more essential than ever. Starting with the first chapter "Do You Hear What I Hear?" we begin to explore whether in the years that have passed, we progressed or actually lost ground.

Pat Gelsinger's insightful prelude to this journey (in his foreword to *Differences That Make a Difference*) encapsulated the spirit of embracing differences as the catalysts for growth and understanding. Today, we reflect on those words with a renewed sense of urgency, as we explore the ways in which the DEI movement has adapted, persisted, and thrived amidst the changing tides of our world. We explore whether we need to change our definitions of inclusion and trust as the work-from-home and hybrid models forever change the world of work. Should the new work environments compel us to look at age demographics and gender through a different lens?

As the authors of this new book unfold the stories of resilience, unity, and progress, we recognize the profound resilience of humanity. The pages that lie ahead reveal the extraordinary ways in which organizations and individuals alike harnessed the lessons of the past to shape a more inclusive future, transcending the limitations that once seemed insurmountable. Yet they also highlight that some of these changes have delayed progress and, in many cases, regressed.

In this sequel, we confront the challenges and triumphs of the post-pandemic world, celebrating the audacity of hope and the enduring power of collaboration. Together, we embrace the nuanced intricacies of what transpired during and after the pandemic, weaving together a narrative that paints the portrait of a society steadfast in its pursuit of justice, equity, and change.

In these pages, you'll find stories of strength, working together, and overcoming obstacles. We'll show you how organizations and people used what they learned in the past to make the future better. This book is all about hope and teamwork, and it shows that we can keep making the world a fairer and better place, no matter what challenges come our way.

ACKNOWLEDGMENTS

Producing a book is a process that refuses to stand aside and let other issues rule the day. And while it would be foolish to describe the days, weeks, months involved as a "life crisis," that time does present a certain kind of winnowing wherein the support of friends and colleagues takes new form, not to mention special importance. And producing *this* book has been especially significant, because we found ourselves *living* the subject.

Our original idea has been transformed by the ideas and contributions of the people whose names appear throughout the book, as well as by the work of our production team. To ascribe to any one of that team only one kind of participation would be to denigrate their work, because each person time after time reached in to improve, to expand, to deepen the message. This team included people of various ages, genders, life experiences, and, of course, points of view.

So a Chicha Morada to the colleagues and family members who encouraged us, and to our team: Julia Ardiles, Pedro Espinoza (father), Dianna Espinoza, Dr. Karina Espinoza, Rachael Garrity, Staci Weber, Emma Welch, and Erin Leong.

ABOUT THIS BOOK

If you just read our "Hello Again" letter, you have—we hope—already experienced one of the core messages on which we are focusing. Mid-read is the phrase *where leaders faltered, death and destruction followed.* Whether you're sitting feet-up, ankles crossed in your cubicle or office, sprawled in front of a fire waiting for the evening news broadcast to launch, or holding your ebook in one hand and stirring the risotto with the other, chances are you react more emotionally than intellectually to that phrase, and that reaction largely derives from how you choose to define the word "leader."

Effective leaders can champion inclusion by fostering an environment that values and celebrates differences. Leaders should actively seek diverse perspectives when making decisions and encourage open communication. Beyond policies, leaders should lead by example, demonstrating inclusivity in their actions and decision-making. By embracing diversity, leaders not only enhance organizational performance but also contribute to a more harmonious workplace.

Whatever else it has done, the pandemic has divided families, companies, communities, countries, and cultures into ideological and political camps, often distorting, if not destroying, the common ground on which we all depend for what this book is about: inclusion and belonging. If you find that being included in one group means you choose to be excluded from another, are you then denying that diversity and inclusion are inevitably interwoven?

We as authors seek to first examine how potential readers will "load" the concept of inclusion/belonging based on their prior learning and experience (all the while admitting, of course, that we do, too) before we focus the lens more closely on how it affects our success in a business setting.

You will find that the sources we cite are themselves rather peculiarly "inclusive" in that they call on much more than the standard institutional research and business reporting. At the same time, this book spends little time and space on data collection and statistical proofs. We found ourselves face-to-face with how COVID has scrambled demographics and other survey data so that prediction can be iffy. Our core effort is focused on creating a platform for authentic idea exchange with and among our readers. This book aims to amplify the voices of leaders who are themselves championing inclusion, while inspiring you to do the same.

So, come in, please. You do belong here.

Author's Note: This book was a collaborative venture. So when we are using "we" it was written by our contributing authors and when we use "I" it was primarily written by Pedro David Espinoza.

You can't build a society purely on interests, You need a sense of belonging.

~ Valéry Giscard d'Estaing

The Real ROI:

Return On Inclusion

CHAPTER ONE

Do You Hear What I Hear?

—

Let's start with the most critical element in communication: the words we use. As someone who moves between two languages regularly, by flying to Lima from Palo Alto every month and doing business in English and Spanish, I'm a firm believer that what we say matters, but how we say it matters the most. It is crucial to be mindful of how we word phrases, how we employ idioms and use colloquialism. Given that I flip between English and Spanish every day, it is truly important to be self-aware of the lexicon we employ. For instance, I remember for the first book, I interviewed 150 CEOs and at the end of the interview, I would ask them: what is the number one trait of a Fortune 500 CEO? Can you guess what they all said in common? Self-awareness. I was stunned. It wasn't EQ. It wasn't how good of a listener one is. It wasn't how great of an eloquent public speaker or salesperson, but it was self-awareness, and being sensitive of one's words, limitations, areas of growth, strengths in order to bring the right people for the right job, to grow the company's mission. Hence, now that we live in the AI age where we consume terabytes of information daily, we must be aware of the words and idioms we use in order to be inclusive leaders. As it turns out, even without the complications involved in moving between languages, or between dialects in one language, when one chooses a word, its meaning, and its message rest solidly with the listener.

Author's Note: We encourage groups who are working through this book to consider these questions? Try asking these questions out loud, if you're reading this book in a book club. We encourage you to not read this alone, bring it to your coworking space, to your office, and be intentional with these questions not only to your colleagues, but also to your direct-reports and managers.

Just for the fun of it, consider the following:

1. What is the difference between calling the young male who empties your wastebasket at work a "janitor" or a "custodian"? Or is the person helping to take care of your elder parent a "caretaker" or "caregiver"?

2. Your friend Joe says his "mom drives a hard bargain." Your friend Marilyn agrees: "My mother does, too." Does your mind's eye see one of those women differently than it sees the other? Which traits would you associate with the description in your mind?

3. If someone behind you in a committee meeting whispers, "Janet really doesn't *belong* here," and you know nothing about Janet's background, experience, or skills, do you conclude she doesn't measure up? Or do you assume a negative value to the person making a comment? Or is Janet simply different? Is difference inherently good or bad?

4. Remember the old jokes about "outstanding in his field" vs "out, standing in his field"? Sometimes there is utter miscommunication born of sloppy wording, itself often an expression of high emotion. A friend of ours recalls a

meeting of young people at her church had some years ago with an incoming pastor. Mini-skirts were the fashion rage at the time, and the pastor wanted to make sure his congregation-to-be understood where he stood: "If I see you in church next Sunday, it had better not be with something on above your knees." Instantly, one young woman cupped her hands, leaned over to her friend, and murmured: "I'm going to get here early with absolutely nothing on above my knees. Want to join me?"

5. Then there are words, often of recent coinage, defined almost exclusively by the point-of-view of the speaker and listener. Take "woke" as an example. A *Wall Street Journal* article in December of 2022 read: "The U.S. Government's Woke Training: Read instructions from the Army, NASA, the VA, and more, obtained via open-records law." If you ask your Great Aunt Nellie what it means, what will she say? Will it matter what color her skin is or what language(s) she speaks? Or if she has any relatives or herself who were part of any of the groups mentioned?

6. If you can, remember how you might have reacted to these words fifteen years ago: insider, diverse, intentional, progressive, belong, inclusion. Are they clothed in more ideology or politics now? Or were they even part of your daily conversation then?

7. In a 2010 lecture on respect delivered at the Woodrow Wilson International Center for Scholars, author and Harvard sociologist Sara Lawrence-Lightfoot called for getting rid of "code labels—'inner-city,' 'at-risk,' 'disadvantaged,' and 'urban'—that mask the racial and economic realities that define contemporary social issues."[1]

The term "Latinx," coined to sidestep gender-specific labels like "Latino" or "Latina," faces significant challenges in gaining acceptance among the very community it aims to represent. According to a 2020 Pew Research Study, a mere one in four US Hispanics are familiar with the term, and less than 3% actively use it. This lack of adoption suggests a disconnect between the term's intent and its reception within the Hispanic community, underscoring the complexity surrounding the usage of "Latinx."

Would you like to know more about Latinx? This article delves into the nuanced history and sheds light on the challenges associated with embracing this linguistic innovation.[2]

8. When you are seeking candidates to fill a specific position and you describe desirable skills or attitudes using words like "ninja" or phrases like "ready to run the bases," is gender bias rearing its head? Or any other kind of unintentional bias? And what are you suggesting about the corporate culture by using those descriptors?

Simply put, if our intent is to include people and make them feel they belong, the first step must be to become aware of how we communicate. We then need to address them and refer to them in ways that are not value laden.

What's more, choosing to personalize routine conversational exchanges is a potent way to indicate you actually see and care about the person you are addressing. Let's say you find yourself in the elevator with Miriam, a recent hire, who tested to be a strong introvert. For the next six weeks she is working mornings only because she has newborn twins at home. You can say, "Hi, Miriam, how's it going?" (Which, of course, you could also say to Antonio, Greta, or Hadip.)

Or you could say, "Hi, Miriam. You look a little tired. Everything okay?" Better? Maybe. It definitely is more personal, but also could be a little threatening, as in the code for "When will all of you begin to show up full-time?" Instead, what about, "Greg told me you have some photos of the twins on your phone. I'd sure like to see them."

Now, check in with yourself. Based on just the words in the paragraph above are you male or female? How about these options—see if you assume you are one gender or the other. How about one age or the other? If so, why?

Greg told me you have pics of the little ones on your phone. I would love to see them sometime if you are interested in sharing. May I see?

My meeting for this afternoon was canceled, so I have a little extra time. Anything I can do to give you a little breathing room?

A friend of ours recounted an experience he had the second or third day he was employed in the public relations department of a trade association. His office was on the same (top) floor as the C-suite, so he took the elevator from the basement parking garage. When a colleague asked if he had met the president, he said, "Not yet," and then admitted he didn't know what the president looked like.

Hearing the exchange, the department receptionist looked up from her desk and said pleasantly: "He was in the elevator with us this morning. He's easy to place because he always stands in the back left corner and looks at the toes of his shoes."

This narrative unveils a potential flaw in the recruitment strategy or the lack of comprehensive introduction to key figures within the organization. On a parallel note, it prompts reflection on whether our friend could have taken proactive steps to familiarize himself with the executive team before joining. The receptionist's casual observation, pinpointing the president's habitual stance in the elevator, underlines the subtle ways in which inherent biases can shape our perceptions and interactions within the workplace, influencing even seemingly trivial aspects like recognizing leadership figures.

With that in mind, let's turn the page back to Miriam.

"Hi, Miriam, how's it going?"

"Fine, thank you."

OR

"Hi, Miriam, how's it going?"

"Thanks for asking. I'm really finding this new project intellectually stimulating."

Inclusion is a two-way street, and a title or lack of one doesn't change the traffic pattern. All too often the message you receive is not the one the speaker (and sometimes the writer) intends. All too often implicit or explicit bias is at work (more on that in another chapter). But not always. Feeling as if you belong involves two kinds of acceptance: from the welcomer and also from the welcomed.

An older friend of ours, who spent most of his professional years as a clergyman, has chosen in retirement to devote a good bit of his time to doing handyman tasks for his friends. Over coffee, recently, he recalled how he had built the skills to do the repairs. "When I was just a little guy," he said, "my grandfather was involved in a project and he called me over by saying, 'Come here, Bobby, I need your help.' Notice he didn't say, 'Come here, Bobby, I want to teach you something.' Quite a difference, isn't there, between being asked in because you are valuable, and being told 'I can make you valuable'?

The woman across the table, also in her 70s, chimed in, "When I was a girl, my mother was focused on making sure I had experience on the domestic front. Each week, I was assigned to iron my father's underwear and our towels—neither of which needed ironing, of course, but the only things she trusted me to tackle." Ah, TRUST, again a chapter coming up.

Remember, words aren't the only carrier of messages. Subtler, but often more powerful, are the tone of voice, facial expressions, and body language.

In their book, *Words Can Change Your Brain: 12 Conversation Strategies to Build Trust, Resolve Conflict and Increase Intimacy*, neuroscientist Andrew Newberg, MD, and Mark Robert Waldman, a member of the executive MBA faculty at Loyola Marymount University, present ways for readers to speak more honestly and listen more earnestly, thereby creating an environment of trust and understanding. They argue that the practice and the use of certain facial expressions can make a material difference. Readers old enough to remember when business telephones were answered by a staff member instead of a virtual agent, can compare this to the standard training technique of suggesting those staff members smile before answering, because the smile usually, subtly, and effectively rendered their tone of voice more engaging and friendly.

"Lead on, Macduff!"
Manic semantics

The famous line, "Lead on, Macduff!" originating from Act 5, Scene 8 of Shakespeare's "Macbeth," is commonly misinterpreted in modern conversations. Contrary to popular belief, this phrase is often misquoted and misunderstood. In reality, the accurate line spoken by Macbeth is "Lay on," which significantly alters its meaning.

The misunderstanding of this phrase is emblematic of how idioms evolve and become embedded in everyday language. People frequently use "Lead on, Macduff!" to encourage or prompt action, assuming it means to inspire or motivate someone. However, the original context in the play depicts Macbeth challenging his adversary to engage in combat. The discrepancy between the intended meaning and its popular usage creates a substantial gap in understanding.

This misinterpretation is a testament to how language adapts over time. As idioms weave their way into everyday discourse, their original context often gets diluted or altered. In this case, the misquotation of the line leads to a misalignment between what was intended by Shakespeare and how it is understood in contemporary language.

The prevalence of this misquote demonstrates how usage often overrides accuracy. People confidently employ phrases without understanding their original context, perpetuating misunderstandings even in casual settings. The evolution of language through such misinterpretations highlights the dynamic nature of idioms and their capacity to shape communication and perception.

So it is, too, with those who use idioms or colloquialisms, or even overly pompous word choices to communicate, knowing full well only those whose backgrounds and current social activities similar to theirs will—another idiom—"get the drift." And the discomfort of the listener is compounded, of course, if they are not fluent in the language in use. Even if it's completely unintentional. As an example, we the authors speak Spanish as a first language, and many of the words we use in Spanish translate into big pompous English words. Take "foment," which we use in Peru quite a bit in our everyday vernacular, but we often must define it when we use it in English business settings. "We want to foment an atmosphere of collaboration and inclusion," only to be asked, what is foment?

This subject was covered briefly in Chapter Nine of *Differences That Make a Difference*, but the issue deserves a second look because today so much communication is carried on with the use of one or another device, which introduces the following challenges:

- It takes extra attentiveness to observe body language even if the exchange includes video. If it's audio only, rustling paper may provide the only clue.

- The playing field is even less level—those who frequently communicate electronically essentially have a "home team advantage."

- Not everyone uses the same channel for what are considered time-sensitive messages or for collaboration. A detailed study of how usage varies by age was conducted by Creative Strategies as reported in the July 2020 issue of *Fast Company*.[3] The same variance applies to online meeting software usage. The pregnant daughter of one of our friends showed her parents the first ultrasound image she received, in which the fetus appeared to cover its ears with its hands. The expectant mother explained only partly facetiously, "It's all those Zoom calls."

Some jargon is itself born of social discrimination, to wit: POSH derives from "port out, starboard home," once the most expensive section of cabins on luxury liners.

Think of the description "well-heeled." What do heels have to do with wealth? And then there is "well-endowed," which in formal usage also signals economic or social wealth, but more commonly refers to the size of certain human body parts.

The list in American usage goes on and on: In like Flynn...in the catbird seat...keep up with the Joneses.... How many come to mind that describes economic or social equity or even parity?

And has this section been just a bit of a struggle to read? Scared to even talk to anyone anymore? That's what happens when the conversation, be it spoken or written, is a collection of words about a subject instead of an exchange of ideas. Inclusion is missing. The writing style of the rest of this book is conversational. Beginning with the "Manic Semantics" subhead, you will find no usage of the words "you" and "we" here. Removing them cuts off collaboration "at the knees."

Consider also how this style dilemma rears its head now on all kinds of screens. The same text can be terse to one receiver and delightfully direct to another. Is X (formerly Twitter) intrepid or insolent? Is Grandpa the only person Beverly communicates with via email? Will you hire an image consultant to enhance the way you look for an online video meeting? How about for the virtual background you use? Does your knowledge of, access to, and ability to afford these services give you a measurable advantage over others who are not using these services?

Finally, a common example amongst the three authors of this book has been the earnest effort of some to relate to us by making a reference to how much they like our culture. Unfortunately, the effort can go awry when the speaker tries to compliment us by highlighting something they love about Mexico. The three of us are from Peru, and while there are many similar elements to our cultures, there are also differences. What we often appreciate how-ever is the effort, and we understand that we have an opportunity to educate. And to make inclusion something acceptable and easy, instead of scary and uncomfortable.

Thus, the takeaway of this "Do You Hear What I Hear?" chap-ter, is AWARENESS in communication. Be aware that what you say might not always be received the way you intend or expect. But please, do not stop trying to communicate! Awareness is simply the beginning, let's talk about how else we can drive toward inclusion in the way we communicate. It is key to remember that each listener has a different background of understanding, one that is shaped by their own unique experiences. It is from that background that we listen, and not from the one of the speaker or writer. Great com-municators account for the background of the listener to ensure their message is heard.

I meant what I said
and I said what I meant.

~ Dr. Seuss

PERSPECTIVES ON POINT

Insights Gained From Personal Interviews by the Authors

KRISTA ANDERSON-COPPERMAN

Krista and I met through Elias Torres, a powerhouse. Elias is the co-founder and CTO of Drift, a Harvard alumnus and super passionate about diversity. Elias and I share the same Christian faith—we met up in my Virginia house when he was driving from Boston to Tampa during COVID. During that time, people preferred to drive over flying for obvious reasons. Elias is a super personable and heartwarming guy. He encouraged me to build my personal brand, my digital brand through LinkedIn. And so it was! In March 2021, I started posting every week on LinkedIn. I posted about my entrepreneurial journey, my failing forward experiences, rejections, successes, wins, losses, my latest angel investments, venture investments and public speaking tips. My LinkedIn profile is where it is thanks to Elias Torres. Since meeting him, that week, I had 800 followers, started posting consistently and today I have 21,000 followers. I gained 20,000 followers in less than two years! Thank you Elias. Krista is a big champion for inclusion and loved the fact that two Latinos in tech became great friends. She was open to sharing her insights on the return on inclusion via a Zoom call. During our conversation, we also talked about the importance of life-work balance and how family comes first. She shared with me about her role as a board member for the Advocates for Survivors of Domestic Violence and how that's really important for her. I cannot agree more with her. If we truly want our employees to feel a sense of belonging at work, we must make sure they have a healthy home, a healthy ecosystem, a safe environment. If we truly want our employees to be themselves and be able to come as they are, let's make sure we ask them real questions about their home situation. Unfortunately, since COVID, anxiety levels have increased, people are stressed, and domestic violence is a real thing. We must take action to solve this problem by first talking about this. Communication is key when it comes to verbalizing and making the issue known. Speaking of communication, Krista was the Chief Communications Officer at Okta. Drift, the company Elias started, and where Krista was a board director, was the world's leading conversational marketing and sales platform that helps businesses connect with customers. Communication is key when it comes to the return on inclusion.

Anderson-Copperman has years of experience in multiple roles at Salesforce and Okta to bolster very informed and informative perspectives on belonging and inclusion. Krista currently serves on multiple boards across diverse domains in the software world. Asana—work management platform, Benchling—biotech research and development software, Cedar—patient experience and payment software and Trove—recommerce software platform. She is a venture partner at TCV and an advisor to multiple high growth B2B Saas companies. In some ways, she defines diversity in her day to day work as she is constantly adjusting to the communication, leadership and cultural styles unique to each company. In my conversation with her, one thing that stood out is her desire to approach each and every organization with a beginners mindset and how doing so can yield diversity of thought, inputs, opinions, and solutions.

Krista leveraged her beginner's mindset to her advantage, excelling in identifying and resolving various challenges. She defined herself as a natural problem solver across all aspects of her life, which seamlessly aligned with her initial role at Salesforce as a customer support representative. Her knack for recognizing and tackling issues within the evolving business environment quickly propelled her into a leadership position in support, acting as a springboard for advancement throughout the organization. Throughout her tenure at Salesforce, spanning fourteen years, Anderson-Copperman held multiple senior leadership roles within the organization, actively shaping a customer-centric strategy that prioritized retention, renewals, and expansion.

Despite lacking an on-premise background upon joining Salesforce, unlike many of her peers, Krista viewed this as an advantage. She remarked,

> **"In many ways, people had preconceived notions or ideas about how things should be done, whereas I didn't. I was able to truly come with a beginner's mind, which served me very well."**

This fresh perspective allowed her to navigate uncharted territories and have an outsized impact on the company's success. Her view is that having that perspective in a leader from both the hiring and personal POV is critical to success in today's ever changing world.

There is institutional wisdom that says, when you have an open leadership role, hire someone who has done this before. In many scenarios, certainly at the top of the organization is the only acceptable option, but I have found, and I talk about this alot in my board and advisory roles, that as you go further down into the organization, taking a look at your top performers across the company and encouraging them to take on new roles and challenges outside of their expertise or current organization almost always yields better results. There is a whole separate chapter on how to do this because it isn't often formalized except in the largest of organizations so I will table that for now and say this isn't new advice— at all—but it always surprises me how few companies do this. It is important because if there is an easy button for adding diversity to a team, this is it.

Every single time I did this in my operating career, I asked the new person coming in to take a beginners mindset. You know our customers, how to navigate the company, and you have an idea or opinion about this team and maybe how things should be done, but I want you to pretend you know nothing and spend your first thirty days asking questions of the team, the supporting players, customers, etc. Your only deliverable for the next thirty days is to come back to me with what you have learned. Every single time, without fail, their preconceived notions were somewhat true, but also proven quite false, which allowed them to be much more creative, thoughtful, and precise in their action plan which ultimately yielded better, faster results. And I think this is the key. We all have preconceived notions about people, or teams, or fill in the blank, but if you spend the time asking questions with an open mind and first principles at the core of your questioning, you will always yield better results. In many ways, it is generic advice that you will read in a self help book or get in therapy. Truth is, time is often of the essence and this approach gets away from us. It takes practice, focus, and dedication to stick to this philosophy in your work both as a leader of IC's and a leader of leaders. From a metrics point of view, practicing this in my career, particularly in hiring, yielded much greater gender diversity in my teams than most of my peers. That is only one piece of the pie but it is a very important entry point.

On the flip side of this, is an individual looking to grow their career? Again, institutional wisdom says up the career ladder is always the better choice over making a lateral move. Not necessarily. Taking a lateral move with the opportunity to learn a different part of the business early in your career is an unpaved yet clear path to much broader responsibility down the road.

We often aspire for the next title, be it Director, VP, etc. but according to Anderson-Copperman, the question you need to ask yourself is

"What do I aspire to do in my career both now and in ten years?"

And that should determine your path. If you are working in product organization and you always want to be in product, by all means, shoot for the Director or VP role in product. But if you want to be the best product leader out there, or if there is a part of you—even tiny—that thinks you might want to do something outside of product, or maybe you aspire to be a C level exec at some point, take the lateral move. You can always go back to product but by taking that lateral moving and employing that beginners mindset, you will grow your career and leadership skills in ways you couldn't have imagined.

SOUHEIL BADRAN

Souheil and I met (and bonded) over sharing the speaking stage at the HITEC Summit in 2021. HITEC stands for the Hispanic IT Executive Council. Every year they host an annual summit in a major city. In 2021, it was in New York. Souheil at the time was COO of Northwestern Mutual and also the executive sponsor of the Hispanic Latin ERG.

When I interviewed Souheil Badran, I could tell he shared the same energy and joy levels as I did. We both shared the term "immigrant hustle" in common. Both of us came to the U.S. at a young age to pursue higher education, received merit-based scholarships and failed forward. We both share a passion for football (soccer) and family values. At the time of the interview Souheil was COO of Northwestern Mutual, a Fortune 100 company. Today, he is the COO of U.S. Bank, the fifth largest bank in the country. He's the COO of the fifth largest bank of the largest economy in the world.

Given his passion for writing, I truly wanted to include Badran's piece of work—please enjoy his LinkedIn article on team building:

How I build inclusive, merit-based teams

A friend of mine recently asked me if organizational leaders should focus on diversity and inclusion or outputs and outcomes. I laughed and told him, "Yes."

In all seriousness, this is a classic case of "both/and." Both efforts are essential to creating true meritocracy in the workplace—an environment where people are evaluated and rewarded based on their talent and performance. And both are essential to an organization's long-term success.

As a leader, it's our job to make sure our workforce reflects the communities we serve, and that our colleagues are inspired to be themselves and ready to perform at their best. But it's not just about creating an environment where diversity is embraced—we need to hold our teams accountable as well, setting high standards and creating a plan to achieve them. Of course, that's easier said than done.

How, why, and the way I lead my teams is guided by what I've learned from my own career, which has taken me around the world. I've seen firsthand what works and what matters most when it comes to organizational leadership to engage teams and build better outcomes.

Creating workplaces where someone can be "Souheil," not "Sam"

In my senior year of college in the late 1980s, I started sending out resumes to employers across the globe. A colleague at the time asked me, "Have you considered changing your first name on your resume from Souheil to Sam?" Unfortunately, disparities and discrimination in interviewing and hiring exist in the U.S. and elsewhere. My friend was worried that if a manager couldn't pronounce my name, it might hurt my chances of being hired. It was never something I considered because I wanted to be true to myself and my heritage. Thankfully, I was able to land that first job—because someone judged me based on my potential to contribute, not on my name. Suffice it to say, I will always be grateful that people saw me as the choice to make, not as a chance to take.

After coming to the U.S. as an immigrant, I worked and lived in Muslim countries as a Christian, and I worked and lived in Europe as a non-European. But I've never felt isolated at work. I've always had leaders and mentors who cared about me and sponsored my development—and I've always felt an obligation to do the same for those around me.

As leaders, we need to embrace people's experiences and backgrounds, and get to know them as individuals. This is what will bring them back for more. This is critical in recruiting, and just as important in retention and development. I'm excited about creating diverse slates of candidates—and we're intentional about the way we work to recruit diverse, exceptional talent. Importantly, we back that excitement up with measurement. We have goals and metrics for both initial and final-round interviews, and it's important to me that we meet these goals.

I'm also passionate about providing brave spaces for people to share their own story and heritage. This has been a north star for how I lead. That's why I believe so strongly in Northwestern Mutual's employee resource groups and my own service as an executive sponsor of our Hispanic Employee Resource Group (ERG). That's also why I feel strongly about organizing team meetings and outings, scheduling one-on-one check-ins with colleagues inside and outside my organization, setting up skip-level meetings with my team's direct reports, and actively participating in as many divisional and company-wide events as I can. The greatest power that any leader wields is his or her humanity. Those human connections keep an organization together.

Encouraging curiosity and ambition

While working to build an inclusive meritocracy, it's important to underscore a message to individual contributors that relationships and careers are a two-way street. Managers are not the only ones tasked with the heavy lifting. All team members need to do their part. Work harder and more strategically than everyone else. Deliver the best-possible results. Demonstrate the value you bring to the table— and do everything you can to get to know the culture, the people and the values of the organization you're joining and embrace them. I mentioned earlier that my work colleagues never allowed me to feel isolated. I never allowed myself to be marooned on an island, either. I've always tried to learn as much as I could about an organization and how it ticks.

I've also tried to do the same with my co-workers. Early on, I met people who loved fishing, so to build relationships, I learned about the sport and went fishing. I even figured out how to clean and prepare the catch for dinner. In my role as Chief Operating Officer at Northwestern Mutual, head-quartered in Milwaukee, I'm often surrounded by Green Bay Packers fans. So, I learned about the game, the team and the players. It sounds simple, but it's too often over-looked. If you expect others to respect and appreciate your unique background, show that same respect for others' interests and passions, too. This is more important than ever as teams and organizations try to navigate a hybrid work environment amid the pandemic. We have to find ways in a 2-D environment to create a 4-D relationship.

We don't have to choose between meritocracy and inclu-sivity. I encourage leaders to approach their role with an abundance mentality and choose to win in both arenas—driving exceptional outcomes for their people and for their customers. As a leader, I ask: are you focusing on these same things? In similar or other ways? Let me know.[4]

On another post on his LinkedIn account, Souheil Badran paid tribute not only to the company's customer service team, but also the teams of service advocates, whom he called "the concierges to our financial advisors," noting that they "help to process claims and payments, provide counsel, and make a human connection—reinforcing the high-quality customer experience we aspire to deliver every day."

To drive the point home, he added:

"And when we do our jobs well, we know that our clients can worry less and live more. That is deeply meaningful work—that's why we frequently and intentionally reflect on the impact we make on people's lives."

Badran reflects that same zeal when he argues that for inclusion to succeed, mentors are important, but not enough. Sponsors are crucial, and a sound way to "pay it forward." As he explains it, a sponsor is in a position to "stretch you beyond your comfort level," building strengths and addressing weaknesses.

Remembering that when he first moved from Lebanon to the United States, several people asked why he didn't change his first name to "Sam," to give himself a clearer path to gaining a good position. "I didn't want to lose my affinity with my culture and heritage," he pointed out, then added firmly he did not wish to be hired because of his background, but for his skills.

Like many of our interviewees, Badran spoke with pride about what many people now call the "immigrant hustle"—the zeal to come to the US to learn, and if at all possible to live the American Dream.

ROQUE BENAVIDES

Roque and I met through his nephew Andres Benavides, Stanford MBA. Andres and I played soccer together in high school in Peru. Passion for real football (soccer) has always brought diverse people together. I want to give thanks to Andres for inviting me to mentor early-stage AI startups in 2017 through the Ministry of Production, while I was CEO of SmileyGo. Later in our careers, I asked Andres to connect me to his uncle Roque Benavides, given his business acumen. In addition to being a writing contributor for *The Real ROI*, Roque was a guest speaker for Pan Peru's Speaker Series, where we fundraised dollars to empower more women to become entrepreneurs in the Andes.

Roque Benavides has fashioned a career—no, better than that, a life—that could easily be considered the paradigm achieving young entrepreneurs might wish to emulate. He originally selected an education curriculum that would prepare him to take over when his father retired from the family fine metal mining business in Peru. Then he tweaked his choices just a bit to broaden his curriculum to include civil engineering and added advance degrees in management. He joined the firm, Compañia de Minas Buenaventura, serving first as CFO, then CEO, and finally chairman of the board, all the while taking active roles in Peruvian business organizations. He also continues the interest of and activity in Peruvian national politics, for which his forebears are famous.

Since the three of us are Peruvian, we know and respect not only the business acumen of Benavides, but also his keen understanding of and attention to the fact that in Peru, as in much of the developing world, mines are quite often in areas where poverty is rife. Benavides' conscious and conscientious leadership is thereby particularly important. Not surprisingly, he brings a similar sensitivity—one might even say empathy—to issues of inclusion, particularly in the case of women. As he expressed it in our interview:

"I believe that women should participate because of their abilities, not because they are women, and in that sense, I believe that they must be valued and, of course, make every effort for them to participate more and more. I think it contributes a lot to the well-being of society."

Benavides expands that point of view to hiring practices in particular.

"In the United States, on the boards of the big companies they are already thinking, of course, of Hispanics, of Black people, of women, of Democrats, of Republicans as well.... Diversity has reached an extreme that doesn't really make any sense.... Jay Lorsch, a professor from Harvard Business School, says that boards, for example, should be made up of profiles and not names, profiles.

The profile has to do with the
members' abilities and not with
the fact that they are a woman
or that they are black or white."

To end with Roque's wise insights, he shared his viewpoint on skill-based diversity:

"Diversity has to be in terms of
skills. The profile has to do with their
abilities and not with the fact that
they are a woman or that they are
black or white...in the end, I think
we are not doing women a favor
when it comes to saying 'I am hiring
you because you are a woman,' it
has to be because of your ability."

MICHAEL BOSKIN

Michael Boskin and I met through my Stanford roommate from 2015: Danny Wright. Danny was a sharp tennis player who majored in economics and computer sciences. Did we play tennis? Yes. Who won? Danny played club tennis at Stanford. He won. I'm grateful he connected me to one of his favorite Stanford faculty members. None the less than Michael Boskin himself. When Boskin and I met, we talked about the new economy, the new normality of hybrid work, companies allowing employees with flexible hours and environments. Boskin added:

> "Many workers have found it desirable to have a more flexible work schedule, as well as you would place. It enables some of them to save money by moving out of Silicon Valley to less expensive areas, or to move home and help their parents, or stay home and share responsibility for children who can't get into school."

I agree with Boskin, allowing our workers to be flexible in terms of schedule and place will enable them to help their parents. I myself, am a caregiver for my mom. Having the ability to work via Zoom, give keynote speeches to hundreds of Fortune 500 leaders via WebEx or Teams is a blessing. I can be closer to my mom and help her with her health endeavors. Many of us have aging parents and children who need extra TLC. If we talk about inclusion, let's include those who are caregivers of loved ones. Moving on, Boskin and I talked about the importance of STEM skills. Coding, math, technology, AI, science, etc. He shared:

> ## "It's very important that the basic STEM skills start early. So, we have a pipeline that makes people ready to go to college and succeed in college."

In my life, I started taking computer classes in elementary school, when I was 6 years old. I remember designing my first website on Macromedia Contribute in elementary school on a Mac. Fascinating times! I totally agree with Boskin on the importance of having basic STEM skills at a young age. Hard skills such as computer science, mathematics, statistics and AI are must-have skills in this new age.

Appropriate or not, when the subject is the economy, there is often a credibility tug-of-war between academics and corporate executives—those who deal in research, trends, and analyses vs those who focus on returns, technology, and acceleration. When we finished our interview with Michael Boskin, we were keenly aware of how important it is to be inclusive of both perspectives, especially if we hope to crosswalk in our focus on the Real ROI between the public and the private sectors. It would be glib to say that Boskin has a foot in each camp—not only glib, but incorrect, since he has only two feet. As CEO of his own consulting firm, T. M. Friedman Professor of Economics and senior

Fellow at Stanford University's Hoover Institution, he "covers" corporate and academic. But then he also serves on multiple corporate boards (ExxonMobil, Oracle Corporation, Shinsei Bank and Vodafone Group).... Impressively speaking, Boskin is the recipient of the Adam Smith Prize and other professional awards. Last but not least, Boskin serves on the Commerce Department's Advisory Committee on the National Income and Product Accounts.

There have been multiple media (business and general) articles, as well as academic theses on the various trends that are expected to have measurable effect on the US economy in the near future. Some directly relate to the *Return On Inclusion*. As Boskin sees them:

1. Until COVID the technology sector saw skilled workers' wage rising exponentially, the demand for unskilled labor is now narrowing the gap between the wages of those with a college degree and those without.

2. Regarding the anticipated effects of artificial intelligence, a well-functioning market economy will adjust.

3. More Hispanics and Blacks are getting college degrees, so there is an expanding middle class, but that is not a solution by itself. It is critical that they get basic STEM education, so they can be trained for jobs to come.

Quotas regarding diversity and inclusion like the one the state of California has just legislated don't make sense, but we DO very much need non-discrimination. Firms cannot survive if they don't have competent people. We need to create conditions in which everyone can thrive.

LUIS UBIÑAS

To summarize all his achievements and accolades, Ubiñas is a Puerto Rican leader from New York who graduated magna cum laude from Harvard in 1985 and got his MBA at Harvard Business School as a Baker Scholar. Luis and I share mutual friends such as Sylvia Acevedo (Qualcomm Board Member), Daniel Trujillo (Chief Ethics Officer at McKinsey), Tony West (Uber CLO) and Michelle Lee (USPTO Director).

Our first dialogue was definitely unique and cut to the chase. Luis wrote to me: "Pedro, I notice you use the phrase BIPOC in your profile. Many Latinas, Latinos and Asians find that phrase pejorative. Imagine describing a room made up of 60% women as a room of men and others. Asians and Latina/os are the majority of people of color and shouldn't be dismissed as 'other.'" He was definitely right, the term BIPOC diminishes Latino and Latina community. I replied asking him for his two cents in regards to the other ways of referring to the latin/o community that have crept in in recent years: people of color and Latinx. He said "People of color is a less bad term than BIPOC, as at least it doesn't diminish us, but remember that our community is spectral and many of us are not people of color. As for LatinX, it is an Americanization. I much prefer Latina/o, which respects our language. We all forget that the term LatinX originated as a term for our non-binary brothers and sisters. It's appropriation as a label for the entire community and also dishonors them. It's going to take all of us working one on one to end the use of these terms that erase us." Ubiñas also shared:

"Pew just did a study on the term Latinx. Only 3% of Latinos use it. 76% of Latinos have never heard of it."

He continued, "What is much more important than these debates over what a community is called, are the actual interests of the community. We are finally seeing real attention paid to the interests of the Latinas and Latinos: education opportunity, economic development—in particular the ability to form and sustain small businesses, public safety. These are the issues that matter to us. Can we support ourselves and our families? Can we educate our children so that their futures can exceed our present? Can we live safely in neighborhoods without fear of crime and violence?" He continued, "Our community, with its large numbers and above average workforce participation, now represents 20% of the workforce of the country. We go to college at above average rates, create businesses at above average rates, we represent nearly half the economic growth of the country because so many of us are in prime household formation years. These are the issues and facts that matter to us."

He closed by pointing to the 2024 election, "there are now more than 36 million Latina and Latino voters. These votes will ultimately go to the Party which best represents the interests of the community. The Party that understands Latinas and Latinos not as part of some amorphous grouping but as a community with clear and specific interests that are distinct from those of other communities."

DAVID PETRAEUS

General David Petraeus and I met through a great friend of mine Sylvana Q. Sinha. David and I are both proud investors of Praava Health, the largest outpatient healthcare system in Bangladesh—founded by Sylvana Sinha. Sylvana and I met at Davos for the Annual Meeting of the World Economic Forum in 2022. When Sylvana and David connected us, we bonded over our passion for discipline, waking up early in the morning, and failing forward principles. During the beginning of our conversation with David, I shared how my mom was very disciplined and methodical: no TV during the week, raised us with no dessert, no caffeine, and with tons of sports (tennis, basketball, soccer, swimming), extra-curriculars (French, Japanese, etc. classes) and arts (piano, guitar, violin, drums, etc.). David agreed with me that discipline is what helps us embrace good habits for our careers and personal lives. He went further by expressing:

"Determination is a quality that most if not all successful people have."

I remember applying to U.S. colleges for the first time, straight from Peru. The first 9 letters were all REJECTION letters. Was I sad? Yes. Was I upset? Yes. Shared the news with my father Pedro—he encouraged me to pray, be patient and carry on. He was right! The tenth and last letter came from Berkeley—and they ACCEPTED me with merit-based scholarships. Wow! Determination—failing forward, pushing, pushing and pushing.

Later in our conversation with General Petraeus, he shared:

"When you are engaged in grueling endeavors...you need to have a pretty big reservoir of determination, resilience, fortitude, and strength."

Given his public image and accolades, we believe David Petraeus doesn't need an introduction: Director of the CIA (Central Intelligence Agency) from 2011 to 2012, United States Army General, Commander of the International Assistance Force and Commander of United States Central Command. Today, David is a Partner at KKR (Kohlberg Kravis Roberts & Co), an American global investment company with $552 billion assets under management. He is the Chairman of the KKR Global Institute, which he established in 2013. As his bio is read on the KKR company website: General David H. Petraeus (US Army, Ret.) (New York) is a Partner at KKR and Chairman of the KKR Global Institute, which he established in May 2013. He is also a member of the boards of directors of Optiv and OneStream, a Strategic Advisor for Sempra and Advanced Navigation, a personal venture investor, an academic, and the co-author (with British historian Andrew Roberts) of "Conflict: The Evolution of Warfare from 1945 to Ukraine" (October, 2023). Prior to joining KKR, General Petraeus served over thirty-seven years in the U.S. military, culminating his career with six consecutive commands as a general officer, five of which were in combat, including command of the Surge in Iraq, command of U.S. Central Command, and command of coalition forces in Afghanistan. Following retirement from the military and after Senate confirmation by a vote of 94-0, he served as Director of the CIA during a period of significant achievements in the global war on terror, the establishment of important Agency digital initiatives, and substantial investments in the Agency's most important asset, its human capital. General Petraeus graduated with distinction from the U.S. Military Academy and is the only person in Army history to be the top graduate of both the demanding U.S. Army Ranger School and the U.S. Army's year-long Command and General Staff College. He also earned a Ph.D. in international relations and academics from Princeton University. General Petraeus taught both subjects at the U.S. Military Academy in the mid-1980s, he was a Visiting Professor of Public Policy at the Honors College of the City University of New York from 2013 through 2016, and he was for six years a Judge Widney Professor at the University of Southern California and a Senior Fellow at Harvard University's Belfer Center. He is currently a Visiting Fellow and Lecturer at Yale University's Jackson Institute, Co-Chairman of the Global Advisory Council of the Woodrow Wilson Center for International Scholars, Senior Vice President of the Royal United Services Institute, and a Member of the Trilateral Commission, Council on Foreign Relations, and the Aspen Strategy Group, as well as a member of the boards of the Atlantic Council, the Institute for the Study of War, and over a dozen veterans service organizations. He is also a LinkedIn Top Voice. Over the past twenty years, General Petraeus was named one of America's 25 Best Leaders by *U.S. News* and *World Report*, a runner-up for *Time* magazine's Person of the Year, the *Daily Telegraph* man of the year, a *Time* 100 selectee, Princeton University's Madison Medalist, and one of *Foreign Policy* magazine's top 100 public intellectuals in three different years. General

Petraeus has earned numerous honors, awards, and decorations, including four Defense Distinguished Service Medals, the Bronze Star Medal for Valor, two NATO Meritorious Service Medals, the Combat Action Badge, the Ranger Tab, and Master Parachutist and Air Assault Badges. He has also been decorated by fourteen foreign countries and he is believed to be the only person who, while in uniform, threw out the first pitch of a World Series game and did the coin toss for a Super Bowl.

> I have not heard our countries
> talk about the Peruvian dream, the
> Mexican dream, or Argentinian dream,
> or the Brazilian dream.
>
> ~ Alejandro Valenzuela | CEO of Banco Azteca

ENDNOTES

[1] https://www.wilsoncenter.org/event/lecture-respect-nourishing-goodness-education

[2] https://www.motherjones.com/media/2019/06/digging-into-the-messy-history-of-latinx-helped-me-embrace-my-complex-identity/

[3] https://www.fastcompany.com/90509588/in-the-new-age-of-remote-work-people-under-30-might-finally-kill-email

[4] Badran, Souheil. (2021, October 5). How I build inclusive, merit-based teams. LinkedIn. https://www.linkedin.com/pulse/how-i-build-inclusive-merit-based-teams-souheil-badran/?utm_source=share&utm_medium=member_ios&utm_campaign=share_via

CHAPTER TWO

The Definition Dilemma

—

Before we go deeper into inclusive communication, we should take a pause and consider the current working definition of inclusion. In working on this book, perhaps the greatest change we found, using our experience with *Differences That Make a Difference* as a baseline, is the amount of attention now being paid to diversity, equity, and inclusion (DEI) as a core issue in the business world, primarily in the US but also globally. Much of the focus currently is on the dangerous tendency to conflate the three into one, instead of recognizing that without inclusion, the other two have little chance of being effective. As Laura Sherbin and Ripa Rashid wrote in their 2017 *Harvard Business Review* article:

Numerous studies show that diversity alone doesn't drive inclusion. In fact, without inclusion there's often a diversity backlash. Our research on sponsorship and multicultural professionals, for example, shows that although 41% of senior level African Americans, 20% of senior-level Asians, and 18% of senior-level Hispanics feel obligated to sponsor employees of the same gender or ethnicity as themselves (for Caucasians the number is 7%), they hesitate to take action. Sponsors of color, especially at the top, are hobbled by the perception of giving special treatment to protégés of color and the concern that protégés might not "make the grade." The result: Just 18% of Asians, 21% of African

Americans, and 25% of Hispanics step up to sponsorship (and 27% of Caucasians).[1]

Sherbin and Rashid go on to note the difficulty in measuring inclusion. As we have pointed out elsewhere, diversity can be counted (albeit erroneously, sometimes, when an "increase" represents only the raw number of a specific group added instead of those in increasingly responsible roles), but as they phrase it: "…quantifying feelings of inclusion can be dicey. Understanding that narrative along with the numbers is what really draws the picture for companies." They illustrate the dilemma with a telling example:

> For example, we worked with a Chile-based firm that would seem to have no problems with diversity. After all, one of their most valued employees is an indigenous Peruvian, a man who is respected, well-paid, and included in the leadership team's decision-making discussions. Yet in a one-on-one interview he confided that he saw no future for his ambitions at that firm. "I know they value me," he said, "but I am an indigenous person, and they are white, legacy, and Spanish. They will never make me a partner, because of my color and background." Conventional measures would never flag this talented man as a flight risk; it's up to the narrative to tell the tale. And that narrative is not going to show up in your standard monthly metrics.[2]

There are two other definitional problems not yet solved in either theory or practice:

1. All too often the focus is on employees only. We need to also consider the leaders and our strategic partners.

To build a complete business case for inclusion requires a wider lens, to "include" contractors, consultants, investors, business and community partners, vendors, customers, or, in the case of many not-for-profits, members.

2. Much of the literature and the work on DEI centers around age, gender, sexual preference, nationality, physical, mental, or emotional challenges, ethnicity, and culture (including religious tradition) as the accepted categories. Ethnicity and gender get an overwhelming amount of attention, of course, but all of these tend to be groupings that are obvious, defined by appearance or behavior. Particularly in our post-COVID culture, marked by what is now considered to be a permanent increase in remote working arrangements for many, new subtle groups will come into play such as employees struggling with the high cost of childcare. Multiple sources suggest it currently tops $1,000 a month per child.

> Those living in areas where access, speed, or both of online communication is sketchy at best—essentially a "techno-desert."

> Those whose value systems render some environments, decisions, and even people at best unacceptable and at worst frightening. The recent dilemma over masking is an obvious case in point.

There have been multiple media articles, as well as academic theses on the various trends that are expected to have a measurable effect on the US economy in the near future. Some are directly related to the *Return On Inclusion*.

Finally, all-too-often overlooked is the assumption that affected groups share at least one thing: without a viable inclusion effort they are, for one reason or another, the "underdogs," blocked from legitimacy, authority, and power. That would, in turn say, no privileged group CEO need to worry. Not so. If a CEO who for whatever reason is not receiving open, timely feedback from colleagues and customers, he or she could suffer from lack of inclusion and his or her company's performance will show it.

In the United States, on the boards of big companies they are already thinking, of course, of Hispanics, black people, women, Democrats, and Republicans as well. Without thoughtful planning and strategically driven goals, however, diversity seems to have reached an extreme that doesn't really make any sense. Jay Lorsch, a professor from Harvard Business School, says that boards, for example, should be made up of profiles and not names, profiles. The profile has to do with the members' abilities and not with the fact that they are a woman or that they are black or white.

In *Radical Inclusion: What the Post-9/11 World Should Have Taught Us About Leadership,* co-authors Martin Dempsey, former chairman of the Joint-Chiefs-of-Staff and Ori Brafman, *NY Times* best-selling author, recall a graduation speech that General Glenn Otis, then commander of the US-Army Europe, delivered at Fort Leavenworth, KS. Pulling a 3x5 card from his pocket, the general said:

> "I carry this card with me at all times to remind me about the most important attribute of a leader. The card reads: 'When is the last time you allowed a subordinate to change your mind about something?'"[3]

If we are to agree that Diversity and Equity cannot exist without Inclusion, then we will also recognize that at the time of this publication we do not have a standard way of defining or measuring inclusion. As a result, we want to highlight here that as leaders, it is important for us to be aware that DEI metrics are numbers that need context. And we need to ensure we have the proper feedback loops so that we can understand what our metrics tell us and expand our perspectives through interactions with those whom we are not typically exposed to.

You would be surprised how crucial it is to include everyone in this journey of inclusion. By everyone, I mean everyone. Many times people think, if we had a female CEO or person of color CEO, things would change. But it isn't that easy. For instance, I've worked with a Fortune 500 company in the Midwest, where they have a female COO, person of color CEO, where the entire leadership team understands the business case, the ROI for inclusion. Nevertheless, they forgot about mid-management. That's where the rubber meets the road. You can have the most intentional and diverse CEO in the top, with an amazing CFO/COO, but, if your middle-managers aren't trained when it comes cultural intelligence, when it comes to inclusion, the women and people of color won't get promoted. Simple enough, we will get the same results. One person can't change the whole company. It takes a team. That's the opportunity I saw while consulting/speaking at this company, and they followed my advice on providing professional development sessions when it comes to being well versed in cultural intelligence. As a result, after six months, over 75% of their mid-managers were culturally smart, and we saw the numbers rise, when it came to female leadership and people of color leadership. They were getting mentored, but most importantly sponsored. By sponsored I mean, people were vouching for them, wearing their jersey when they were not present: boardroom, hiring room and promoting room.

Recognize yourself in he or she who are not like you or me.

~ Carlos Fuentes

PERSPECTIVES ON POINT

Insights Gained From Personal Interviews by the Authors

GREG BUCHERT

Perhaps at no time in the last century has well-conceived and delivered healthcare been more important in the US and globally. In a series of organizations and roles—CEO, physician, consultant, investor (both angel and venture), startup advisor, community advocate—Greg Buchert has experience in the field that is both broad and deep. Currently CEO of GSB Health Management Solutions, a consulting and advisory services firm that focuses on innovative solutions, he begins our interview by noting that there is no universally accepted measure of "success." Then he offered a story:

> A man participating in a program designed to help parents cope with disabled children comes in for a "talk." He confesses he has hated his wife since their child was born. And he has expressed that hate by substance abuse and multiple extramarital affairs. Now, finally, he realizes that he, not his wife, not his child, is the problem.

Equity, and thereby inclusion, Buchert insists, rests on that kind of realization—one that says: "I may never agree with you, but I can and will try to understand you."

MELANIE COOK

Relationships. Relationships have helped me tremendously to achieve, dream and attain. The famous Harvard Business Analytics program (HBAP) opened doors for me during my mid 20s. One of the first classmates I met at Harvard was Jose Lopez Reynoso (MIT MBA, Director of Data at GE Appliances). We bonded over our Christ-centered faith, family values and sports. He looked me up on TED and LinkedIn—he loved my TED Talk! He opened doors with the Inclusion and Diversity Leaders at GE Appliances to see if there was a fit. Wow! Not even one week done of this HBS program and here we are closing business deals. Super grateful for Jose. He also connected me with Melanie Cook, the COO of GE Appliances at that time. Melanie and I clicked with many areas in common: Florida affiliations, love for traveling, the outdoors, appreciation for family, cultivating relationships and fostering strength in our communities. In 2022, I participated in three speeches/conferences in Michigan, I remember sharing that with Melanie given that she has roots there too. When it comes to relationship-building, I've always found it fascinating to see how easy it is to connect with people when you reach out to them: hey I'll be in this state/city, you told me your parents/siblings live here! Any recommendations? Things like that go far. People remember the small details and appreciate the personal connection. As a result of these connections, GE Appliances invited me to speak during their Annual Summit on Inclusion and Diversity. It was an honor for me to speak to over 900 GE Appliances employees worldwide. So far, I think it's been one of the largest live audiences I've had. Super grateful! Thank you, Melanie.

When Melanie Cook retired as chief operating officer of GE Appliances, a position she had held for four years, the letter from GE Appliances president and CEO Kevin Nolan read a little differently from the norm. In addition to cataloging her contributions during her tenure with the company, he wrote: "Melanie has been a friend and mentor to so many employees who appreciate her strategic vision, her counsel and her laughter." I truly agree with Kevin, during my interactions with Melanie—she is a very kind, supportive and heartwarmingly friendly human being but also intensely passionate.

In our interview with Cook, it became clear that her "strategic vision" was articulated in real-life, regularly scheduled ways. Conceding that sometimes affinity groups ("Most belong to more than one") can become exclusive instead of inclusive if they fail to focus on the goals and culture of the overall organization, she noted that GE Appliances instituted standing pulse meetings. They met three times a week with a diverse cross-functional team and visuals to move from identifying a problem to finding a solution with all "hands on deck" for the most pressing challenges or opportunities. The standard questions posed were: "What is the definition of the problem/opportunity we are facing? What can we do about this? What are we learning? Where are the gaps?" Creating a culture where inclusion is a way of working and everyone feels heard and appreciated makes the difference in finding a mediocre solution or finding an optimal solution in an optimal amount of time.

A common mission, she stresses, provides room for people from different cultures and domains, with different perspectives and expertise, to be able to participate freely, and even say "no" when that's their sincere reaction.

Not one to sit idly by Melanie has formed a firm—M.E.L. BIZ LLC— (Motivate.Empower.Lead.) that is multidirectional, focusing on Corporate Director roles, advisory services, and non-profit leadership. Today, Melanie serves on the Board of Directors of Commercial Vehicle Group, Inc. (NASDAQ: CVGI), Badger Meter, Inc. (NYSE: BMI), Thetford Corporation, a Monomoy Capital Partners Company, and The Legacy Companies bringing her Global Cross-Functional Leadership to the Board Room. She is a Trustee on the board of Family Scholar House, a non-profit whose mission is to end the cycle of poverty through education. She is also an Executive Advisor to Bruviti, an AI Tech Company focused on Service Operations.

CAROL CHRIST

We have lots of company when we say we admire UC Berkeley Chancellor Carol Christ for her "firsts,"—first woman in that role being but one of many. She would, we know, prefer to talk about "foremosts"—her trademark intensity about building programs that advance the missions and recognize the people contributing to the common good. A recent welcome message she penned makes that clear:

> The University of California, Berkeley is a place of immense intellectual vitality, where some of today's brightest students and scholars work together to deepen understanding of the world we live in. It is also a place that is steadfastly committed to widening the doors to educational opportunity, a place that sets young people from all backgrounds on a path towards success in their lives and in their careers. This combination of excellence and access is what defines and animates us; it is truly Berkeley's DNA.

And for those of you who are beginning to believe that for authors of a book about diversity, we are hopelessly California-centric, may we add that Christ spent more than a decade at Smith College. Among her achievements there was the supervision of the development of an accredited engineering program, the only one at a women's college in the US.

In our interview, Carol repeatedly stressed that any institution seeking to serve all members of the community in which they operate or plan to operate needs to insist that someone who can speak for under-represented groups be not only at the decision-making table but able to articulate their points of view but be heard—in other words included. "That's the only way the remainder of the group at the table can actually see things different ways," she concluded. And speaking directly to the subject of collaboration between universities and the private sector she strongly supported internship programs.

While Carol and I were talking about understanding the experiences of the underrepresented communities, she brought up this quote:

> "But who is at the table changes the angle of a particular conversation. So we try at Berkeley to apply an equity lens to all our decision making. And that's much easier to do if you have someone who understands the experience of the underrepresented members of our community."

Sometimes, cold emails go a long way. Given that I still have my Berkeley.edu email account, I decided to cold email the new chancellor of Berkeley, Carol Christ. In my email I referenced a few of the Berkeley alumni I had worked with for my first book (*Differences That Make a Difference*) such as Eric Schmidt, Joe Simitian and Maria Weaver. I asked Carol for a ten minute interview to gain her thoughts on the return on inclusion. She said yes!

I cannot agree more with Carol, the Chancellor of my Alma Mater, when she refers to who sits at the table modifies the angle of a particular conversation topic. Her words brought a smile to my face. It's the same feeling I have every day, when I start a board of directors meeting at an AI startup company in San Francisco, when I'm attending the Annual Meeting in Davos by the World Economic Forum, when I am attending a Forbes 30 Under 30 Forum in Ireland, when I'm speaking at Davos, when I'm delivering a keynote speech to 900 employees for a Fortune 500 Company in San Jose, CA. I'm smiling because I get to represent my Hispanic community at these places and that, definitely, applies an equity lens to the decision making at these power networks. It's not just access to capital, but also access to network. And this, we must change for people of color and women. Later in our conversation, we talked about the power of real-life experience such as internships. I shared with Carol how, as a freshman, I applied to Deloitte, Apple, McKinsey, JP Morgan and others, however, I had zero network. No one referred me. Hence, I got tons of rejections. That motivated me to study engineering at a Stanford program. That's where my first AI startup was born! I founded SmileyGo at age 19! Carol's point on internships were:

> "I think what would be really helpful is internship programs that are specifically targeted at women and underrepresented groups…. Internships are so amazing as opportunities in terms of giving people experience, making them competitive for jobs."

JULIE CULLIVAN

Choose a known corporate name in the tech world; then choose a date within the last thirty-five years. Now, say the name "Julie Cullivan." You'll hear, "Of course, she's great. She was vice president of...." The list is testimony to a career arc that's hard to match: Oracle, Asera, Dell, McAfee, Autodesk, FireEye, and Forescout. The fields include sales, marketing, business operations, field operations, people and technology. And in recent years Cullivan's skills and experience provide valuable insights for her service on multiple boards of directors as well as in advisory roles—for the likes of Cobalt.io, Brighton Park Capital, AaDya (A-Day-A) Security, OPSWAT, SADA, HeartFlow and Axon.

On inclusion on boards:
> "The more inclusionary you are, the easier it is to find diverse talent and experience. Women find and attract other women, etc. Also, it's important that board members have experience serving on pre-IPO boards. When you see yourself as ready to take a board seat, it's important to spend time and effort educating yourself on what it means to be a board member, essentially to develop board sense."

Julie's value in both operational and advisory roles derives not only from the breadth of her experience, but the fact that one of her areas of concentration has been cybersecurity. Her perspective on the return on inclusion is—unsurprisingly—forthright, practical, and clearly productive of both early and lasting results.

> ## "One should not overthink what is meant by inclusion, we learn what it means when we are very young and immediately understand the joy in bringing others into the circle."

On inclusion in the workplace: Be very careful of pattern-matching. Each of us is an individual, who wishes their ideas to be heard. The upfront value of inclusion is the introduction of new ideas.

> ## "Being willing to share a new, different take is completely dependent on feeling it's safe to do so."

We live in an era inundated with the mindset of: A/B testing, B/C testing, Y/Z testing. And I agree, it's crucial for us to MOVE FAST. To adapt, to change, to be flexible and go with trial and error. That's the Silicon Valley way, isn't it? Launch the product. Customer acquisition. Try different user acquisition strategies, execute, deploy, push code! I've been living in Palo Alto the last eleven years. Trust me, I know. However, it's also IMPORTANT to look at things differently, than rush on to trying a distinct method. Let's stop rushing all the time to try a different approach and look at results differently. That's when my good friend Julie Cullivan shared in our interview:

> "You got to be really careful with pattern matching and you really ought to be looking out. Maybe there's a better way...the outcome might have been positive before but maybe you get an even better outcome if you were willing to look at things differently and try a different approach."

I 100% agree with her. We have to be keenly aware about pattern matching. There could be risks! In my second software startup (Skawlar), I co-founded it with my good friend from Princeton—Richard Zhang—I remember I rapidly wanted to change our pricing model. It was a B2C tech startup. I was all about changing prices, modifying the mechanisms immediately, because the results were decent. But I wanted excellent results. That's when Julie's quote came to mind. Don't immediately change the approach, first look at things differently.

RALPH DE LA VEGA

I have to give credit to my great Cuban friend Yovany Jerez for connecting me with Ralph de la Vega. Yovany and I met at The Alumni Society, where I was a guest speaker on Failing Forward. We bonded over our love for Cuban food such as La Carreta in Miami and Pollo Tropical. Ralph is a ball of energy, charismatic and full of passion. Today, he serves on the board of directors of American Express, New York Life Insurance Company, Amdocs, Outreach and Ubicquia. Our interview with Ralph de la Veja, former vice chairman of AT&T and champion of all projects and people described as "entrepreneurial,"—especially in his case Junior Achievement Worldwide where he served as chair—was rich with shared ideas and memories. The three of us grew up in Peru; de la Vega recounted experiences both memorable and menacing about his work introducing cellphone service in South America. And then there is his own boyhood as he describes it:

> "Life is a journey. It doesn't matter where you start. The only thing that matters is where you end up and what you accomplish along the way. My journey as an immigrant who reached the shores of this great country without his family, without speaking the language and without any money, is chronicled in the book *Obstacles Welcome*. It is a story of inspiration for all and proof that the American Dream is still alive. My grandmother (my abuela) served as an inspiration for me when she told me: 'Ralph don't let anyone put limitations on what you can achieve.'"

Ralph clearly believes that new ideas, solutions and progress are born of engagement practiced by people who feel comfortable being together, no matter how different they are. As he writes:

"The difficult challenges that we face around the planet require diverse solutions that incorporate different perspectives and realities."[4]

SHELLYE ARCHAMBEAU

Shellye and I met through a wonderful friend and older sister: Sylvana Q. Sinha. Sylvana and I met at the World Economic Forum Annual Meeting in Davos in 2022. Since then, we hit it off. We opened our networks to each other, I invested in her health tech company, we opened doors for one another. Shellye is a power house. She's on the board of directors of Verizon, Nordstrom and other major multinational companies. She served as CEO of MetricStream for years in Silicon Valley. When we talked about board representation, Shellye mentioned:

"Every board I serve on is a diverse board, and it's not an accident. So it takes being intentional."

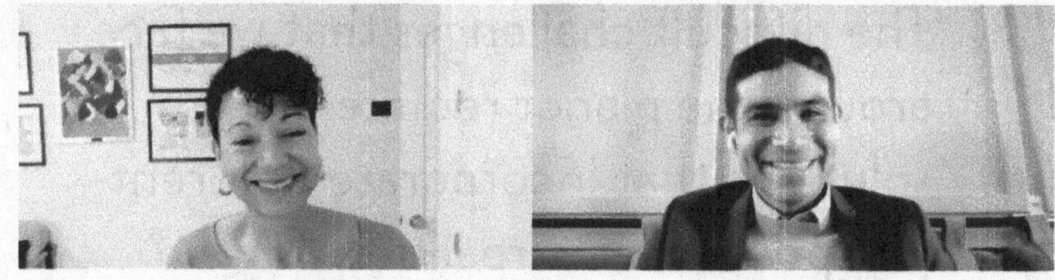

"Diversity means that you want to make sure that whatever environment you're operating in or building or creating, that you have a diversity of everything of thoughts and experiences of ideas and backgrounds."

Pursuing this further, when I asked her about the meaning of inclusion, Shellye said:

"Inclusion means that people feel like they belong...diversity is inviting people to the dance, and inclusion is asking individuals to dance."

ALEJANDRO VALENZUELA

Alejandro and I met at the Hispanic Leadership Summit of 2021 by the We Are All Human Foundation in New York. Claudia Romo Edelman (*Differences That Make a Difference* contributor) put us in touch. Alex and I bonded over our LOVE for tennis. He was a high school tennis star, junior champion in Mexico. He challenged me to play in Mexico City! Who won? We shall see. Anyway, since then, Alex and I have been great friends. Banco Azteca has supported Pan Peru, our 501c3 nonprofit that empowers women to become entrepreneurs (*www.alpacapanperu.com*). We even did a Speaker Series on Inclusion and Innovation to support Pan Peru. Of course, later on, Alejandro connected me with his friends such as Alfredo Thorne—Peru's Minister of Finance.

During my conversation with Alejandro Valenzuela, we talked about access to capital, education, and network. He said it's really hard to pursue entrepreneurship when you don't have equitable access to these factors. I completely agree with him. The United States has a great legal system, entrepreneurship ecosystem and technology infrastructure. In addition to our educational system with top institutions such as Berkeley, Stanford, and Harvard.

"Another main problem that we have in the United States is that the Hispanic community has not been able to develop a common denominator among every one of them. We see an Afro-American population that is more solid. You see the Asian population is also more solid, and the Hispanic community could have a lot more weight in the economic, social, and political matters is still very marginated. We do not know how to work collectively. That is something that we need to work on."

We also talked about the differences of starting a tech company in the U.S. versus a Latin American country. Without a doubt, we both agreed that Latin entrepreneurs embrace more grit and tenacity given that they have to go through political and social turmoil many times. Latin American countries have been through political and social challenges the last decade, starting with Argentina and ending with Chile. Hence, starting an AI startup is way more challenging in LATAM, yet, it is more rewarding. Founders need to embrace resilience to fail forward.

The Political class is changing the country every time. How do you want to have a start-up when we have this differentiator? It makes it very difficult.

~ Alejandro Valenzuela | CEO of Banco Azteca

ENDNOTES

[1] https://hbr.org/2017/02/diversity-doesnt-stick-without-inclusion

[2] https://hbr.org/2017/02/diversity-doesnt-stick-without-inclusion

[3] Dempsey, Martin E., and Ori Brafman. Radical Inclusion: What the Post-9/11 World Should Have Taught Us about Leadership, p. 150. Nakskov: Nota, 2021.

[4] https://www.linkedin.com/pulse/making-world-better-place-ralph-de-la-vega/

CHAPTER THREE

Counting Out the Years

—

When we first began working on this book, our plan was not limited to, but most definitely taken as one *raison d'etre,* the opportunity to showcase the strides US business leaders had made in DEI and the payoffs they (and us) are enjoying—hence the title. Then as the tentacles of COVID began to squeeze out traditional practices—who worked when, with whom, for how long—even the best-planned DEI programs and processes required attention. It became apparent that even well-funded, artfully articulated DEI programs were falling short.

Age is a resounding example. Today, arguably for the first time, five distinct generations populate the workplace. Not all sources agree on the specific age ranges, but with some minor variations the taxonomy from oldest to youngest is as follows: Traditionalist (also sometimes called the "Silent Generation"), 76 and older; Baby Boomer, 57 to 75; Generation X, 41 to 56; Millennial 26 to 40; and Generation Z, up to 25. Of course, until recently, we weren't in the business of describing generations by studying how the behaviors and values of each group differ from the others. Still, a growing amount of scholarly investigation argues that the behavioral and ideological differences between the generations *matter.* Despite that, according to a recent Harvard Business School report, only 8% of US corporations consider "age" as fitting within their DEI-affected groups. Is that a dangerous oversight? Arguably, 75 percent of all purchasing decisions today are made by millennials, are they well represented in our companies? Are they included and have a sense of belonging?

A recent commotion regarding inner-office emails between IBM execs could be characterized as the canary in the coal mine. As reported in the *Boston Globe*, one message calls for a strategy that will "accelerate change by inviting the "dinobabies [new species] to leave," and in so doing to become extinct. Another, apparently referencing older female employees, calls for getting rid of the company's "dated maternal workforce" because they fail to "understand social or engagement. Not digital natives. A real threat for us."[1]

Insisting that such phrasing "does not reflect company practices or policies," IBM spokespersons denied any age bias. Indeed, an IBM website entitled "Be Equal" promotes "Allyship," and reports there are (in 2021) 13,000 IBMer mentors and coaches.[2]

Obviously, even with published core values and well-established systems to support and articulate those values, it takes time to build consensus among management ranks. Contributing author, Pedro David Espinoza points out, though, that the companies with which he has worked, such as Oracle, Cisco, AT&T, Bristol Myers Squibb, and UBS have been able to create age-based Employee Resource Groups that can enhance peer-exchange and often head off potential problems better than top-down communication.

In March 2022, "The Big Idea Series" of *Harvard Business Review* focused on what the developers called "Getting the Best Out of the Five-Generation Workforce."[3] One study entitled "Harnessing the Power of Age Diversity" illustrates the fact that, as we mentioned earlier, few US organizations include age in their DEI strategies, and that those who do often either deny there are generational differences or do little other than to encourage the various generations to put emphasis on their similarities. So, what do the authors recommend? A full explication of what they refer to as a "framework" is found in their book, *Gentelligence*.[4]

The first two of four practices in the framework deal with eradicating false stereotypes and the last two with developing both the willingness and the ability to enrich mutual understanding.

Another study in the same series, "How Shadow Boards Bridge International Divides," is authored by two colleagues from IMD, who spent five years studying shadow boards (groups of young, non-executive employees who work with the executive board, bringing new perspectives to inform the development of strategies). Their research involved organizations as small as twenty-five or fewer employees to as large as 200,000+ in multiple countries. The authors spell out both requirements and pitfalls, concluding that shadow boards, organized and operated competently, can "put management's finger on the pulse of the organization while also keeping its eyes on the future."

Like age defined groups, there may be other groups in your company or organization that may need attention. The superpower of inclusion is seeking understanding, and that starts with asking questions and exposing yourself to new groups and new experiences. As noted before, employee resource groups in large companies are a great way to get involved with established groups that have organized and have a mission behind them. For smaller businesses that may not have ERGs, start your own way to bring others together. Contributing author, Maria, shared that AT&T had a grassroot effort called "DINE" in which small groups of 5 people of very different backgrounds went to dinner with a clear intention to seek to understand each other better. The ground rules were simple: humbly open to share with authenticity and sincerity your experiences, while no judgment be made at the table by others. This allowed for a dinner in which tough questions were asked and answered, and people grew in understanding and respect of each other.

Author's Note: If you are going through this book together as a company, take this time to review your company's lists of ERGs or even provide a copy of that list when you distribute this book to employees. Feel free to send it to the board members of the ERG in addition to the executive sponsor of the ERG. Many times, at large companies, ERGs have an executive sponsor, someone who's in the C-suite leadership team who has some affiliation to the ERG. You don't have to be to belong. We've seen non-Hispanic executives be the executive sponsor of the Hispanic ERG.

When contributing author Jorge Titinger was an operating CEO, he had a practice to hold "lunches with Jorge" wherever he traveled in the world and held them monthly in the USA. These lunches were with fifteen to twenty employees, carefully selected to represent different functional areas, different levels, and diverse by design. There was no agenda, other than to bring up to the CEO areas where people thought the company could do better. At the beginning people were nervous about attending these lunches, but as word got out and several of the ideas were implemented (with the proper credit to the person who brought it up), employees began to want to participate, and their sense of belonging increased. Trust between leadership and teams evolved during these lunches and strengthened while the employees' ideas were being implemented. Another huge benefit for the company was that the CEO would be made aware of several issues (many of them apparently minor, but meaningful to the employees) that would not have shown up through "normal" channels. Significant improvements in inclusion and belonging take time, perseverance, and action.

Be sincere. Be simple in words,
manners and gestures.
Amuse as well as instruct.
If you can make a man laugh,
you can make him think and
make him like and believe you.

~ Al Smith

PERSPECTIVES ON POINT

Insights Gained From Personal Interviews by the Authors

MICHAEL DELL

I have to give credit to my mentor, friend and brother Pat Gelsinger for this one. Pat graciously connected me with Michael in 2020. As we shared in our first book, Pat and I met in 2018 and immediately connected over our Christian values: generosity, joy and thankfulness. He gifted me a signed copy of his book—*Juggling Act*—which inspired me to write my own book. A year later, in 2019, Pat wrote the foreword of my first book. Prior to being the Intel CEO, Pat was the VMware CEO. VMware's parent company was Dell. I remember Pat's peculiarity of chances "2/3 chances that Michael will say yes and 1/3 chances that Larry Ellison will say yes to an interview." Hence, when I started writing my second book—Pat kindly put me in touch with Michael Dell. Michael and I hit it off via our Zoom interview. I shared how one of my first memories with technology was turning on a Dell computer when I was 5 years old. I thanked him for his vision, for his inventions, and for innovating our world. Surprisingly, he mentioned he'd never been to Peru (out of the many countries he's visited). Years later, after our first conversation—I ran into Michael at Davos for the World Economic Forum. He recognized me! Remembered my full name, country of origin, mutual friend, company name (Pan Peru) and what I did to support rural women in the Andes to become entrepreneurs. I was impressed by his memory! Michael probably meets thousands of humans per year. Yet he remembered me! Made me feel special. The power of inclusion—by memorizing one's names and backgrounds. Memorizing your audience's teammates' names always goes the extra mile. Kudos to you Michael!

In May 2021, when Michael Dell took the stage to deliver the keynote address in Dell Technologies' second virtual conference, he was not hesitant to laud technology for its key role in preventing economic disaster during the pandemic age. As he put it:

> "I stand here, grateful for our role
> in keeping your organizations up
> and running and delivering for
> your customers. For your patients,

your students and your citizens. Together, we prevented a complete societal economic meltdown; that isn't hyperbole. It's what we as technologists did for the world since the shutdowns begin. It was the culmination of decades of work, combined with a burst of innovation, reinvention, reengineering, that has been incredible."[5]

Michael Dell's experience both in the corporate world and the non-profit arena (the Michael & Susan Dell Foundation he and his wife formed in 1999 has as its mission the improvement of education, health and safety for children around the world) comes to the fore in a brand of leadership that is at once decisive and persuasive.

His view of virtual/remote/hybrid work:

"People who never imagined they could work from home quickly realize that work isn't the place. It's an outcome that they can achieve from anywhere, and they like it."

"It's good for your people and good for your company. People are flipping the narrative on the work-life balance. It's now life-work. As a company, we're able to move faster, make decisions faster, respond to you faster, and make changes faster inside our company. We can open the aperture on talent without geographical limitations and engage underrepresented populations and communities around the world. Greater diversity means a broader perspective."

In our discussion of the tangible steps that CEOs and other senior managers can take to promote inclusion of all affected groups in a virtual office setting, Dell points out that this is not a completely new need, noting that his company focuses on "creating space for everyone to show up and to be their authentic selves." One example is what he calls "virtual listening sessions" for affected groups.

Already well-known for the strength and influence of its Employee Resource Groups, Dell Technologies puts special emphasis on the need for senior managers to "show up" for ERG meetings not only to reinforce the work that the ERG itself is doing, but also to encourage, enable and empower collaboration among the groups.

13 ERGs
with more than 469 chapters in

80 geographic locations
across four regions.

In FY24, 56.4% of employees
participated in at least one ERG.

Successful strategy? Something is working and working well. In 2020, Dell shipped ninety-nine PCs every minute, every day.

CAROLINE DORSA

Caroline and I met through my outstanding friend Jesus Mantas. Love his first name. Jesus and I have a passion for tennis. I was a guest speaker at IBM for the Hispanic Jam in 2021. Jesus and I clicked over family values and integrity principles. He introduced me to the outstanding Caroline Dorsa, a class act.

Caroline Dorsa's expertise in finance and her management skills have produced a successful career in not one, but three segments of the US economy—technology (Avaya, Inc.); pharmaceutical (Merck) and utilities (Public Service Enterprise Group Inc.) And that's just the operational side. She currently serves on the boards of directors of Intellia; Biogen, Inc.; Illumina; and Duke Energy Corporation.

Building on that experience, Caroline has strong opinions about how to increase what might be called the "inclusion complement" on corporate boards. She has no patience with the excuse that claims "We just couldn't find anyone appropriate." If the slate is diverse enough, she argues, the choice will be diverse. What's more, she offers tangible ways of creating a diverse slate. Anyone tasked with finding board members whose own network is not sufficiently diverse needs to find someone else whose network is. When appointees are different—not just gender, but points of view defined by other heritages or experiences—employees who resemble those appointees think "that could be me," and their attitudes about their employer and their own "belongingness" change accordingly.

During our interview, Caroline shared about how crucial it is to have a diverse pool of candidates:

"You require diversity in the candidate pool always. And then what happens is you end up with diversity in the selection."

I couldn't agree more. Demographics at top universities are changing. Ten years ago you couldn't expect to have a diverse slate of candidates if you only searched for talent at a Stanford, Berkeley or Harvard. Moving on, Caroline and I talked about the power of not planning everything:

"I think people who've tried too hard to plan their lives miss so much because they don't let their lives take them where fortune takes them."

Wise words from Caroline. Lastly, we talked about the importance of mentorship to get more women and people of color in leadership:

"I developed people.
I identified leaders early....
That's the way you pay it forward."

Those were Caroline's words when it came to developing the next generation of leaders. Thank you Caroline!

HENRY FERNANDEZ

> "I think that there've been a number of chapters in the evolution of my life to get to the point in which I am a strong believer in diversity and inclusion."

I can't agree more with Henry on this one. As a strong believer in cultural intelligence, it is key for the 21st century leader, for the AI era leader, to be well versed in inclusion.

"We are going to be one people working for one cause, going in one direction. And all of that is going to be a huge benefit to the company because we're going to get so many different points of view, so many diverse."

Getting different viewpoints from diverse folks is what makes a team creative and innovative. I can't agree more with Henry on this one. Uniting diverse teammates for one common goal. Like he shared in his previous quote, we need to take risks. Life is full of surprises. Literally. How did I become the Vice President of the Silicon Valley Leadership Group? Every year, I get invited to speak during Hispanic Heritage Month at different companies, organizations, and universities. It was in September of 2021, I was 26 years old, when my friend Anna Dapelo Garcia invited me to be the keynote speaker for Stanford Healthcare's Hispanic Heritage Month. This was a hybrid event where the speakers were present in Palo Alto. Using my culturally intelligent skills, I befriended one of the executives given that her daughter played for the Stanford Division I varsity team. In addition, I bonded with their CEO David Entwistle given that his son had done a mission trip in Chile sharing the gospel. So many things in common! During the event, the Dean of Diversity at Stanford Medical School, Dr. Reena Thomas, and I bonded over our Hispanic Heritage. She briefly mentioned her husband was the new President CEO of SVLG. I said: small world! I used to serve on the CEO advisory task force committee in 2018. A few days after the speech, Reena reaches out asking me to connect with her husband Ahmad Thomas. At the time, I was visiting Seattle when we all connected over Zoom.

Ahmad was direct—he offered me a six-figure VP role in Silicon Valley. I became the youngest vice president at the Silicon Valley Leadership Group in history. With the biggest paycheck too. That's how the VP of business development story came about! You never know how or when, so it's important to be on your feet, ahead of the game and ready to relate with others.

> ## "Life is about going out and talking and being open and getting to know people, taking some risks."

100% with Henry on this one. My parents encouraged me to go out of the house, befriend people, offer to shake hands, offer a smile. I remember in 2009 when we moved homes within Lima, that I didn't have park friends. This new house, while smaller, was next to a park with a soccer field. During high school, I was a total nerd. LOVED reading books, staring at maps, solving mathematical equations and derivatives. My dad said "PD go out! Make some friends at the park! You can't be a ratón in the biblioteca." He literally took me to our home's main door, and said "anda hijo! Vamos! Tu si puedes! Con Dios." Next thing? I befriended many kids in our park, joined their soccer pickup games, became "el men del momento" thanks to my quirky humor, silly jokes and hilarious soccer tricks: I decided to put unique and hysterical nicknames to all my park friends. We were the kids next door!

"The virtual world gave a lot of those people a democratizing process. They now had an equalizing process of having the same information... that created a leveling of the playing field and a democratizing process that people love."

When we talk about the positive externalities of the pandemic, it definitely helped the introverts in the office! Prior to COVID, if you were an introvert it was harder for you to leave your office cubicle and knock on the door of your colleague to ask for advice. It was harder for the timid person to jump out of their seat to approach her boss' cubicle to ask for a raise. It was way more difficult for the shy, common Joe to step out of his comfort zone while in the big tech cafeteria to ask the employee next to him about "what nonprofit boards do you serve on? I want to join boards." The playing field has leveled to some extent, thanks to COVID. Now all you have to do is reach out to your coworker via Teams/Slack. You don't have to grab the mic. All you have to do is send a LinkedIn message or create an email to ask for advice. I encourage you, dear reader, to be intentional and reach out to a coworker, direct report or supervisor to ask for advice, perhaps you want to join a nonprofit board, advisory board or change business teams. You never know how, you never know when.

I first heard of MSCI through a fellow Berkeley Haas student. The Berkeley Haas library is known for not having too many study lounges. Hence, students had to fight over them. I would use my charm, my smile and simpatía to convince students to let me use the study lounges. One day, a week before finals, I was studying with my Haas buddies when we realized we hadn't reserved the lounge. Two older MFE (Masters in Financial Engineering) students had reserved the study lounge—Daniel Barrera and Oscar Alban. They knocked on the door with the intention of kicking us out. They had the right. Nevertheless, I took advantage of the opportunity to befriend them. I rapidly found out they were Latino: Oscar is Colombian and Daniel is Mexican. Hablamos Español! We immediately started talking in Spanish, I shared a Spanish joke, we were all cracking up. Long story short, they let me stay in the student lounge. I added them on LinkedIn. Next week, Daniel finds out I'm a tech founder and invites me to speak at MSCI—the company he was interning at. Thanks to Daniel, I was a guest speaker for MSCI when I was a 20-year old tech founder in Berkeley. I spoke about the future of machine learning and how SmileyGo is using data science to empower Fortune 500 companies to give/invest smarter. We were using AI for good, AI in philanthropy. Wow! Times flies. Anyway, after that, I got invited to speak at MSCI a few more times both locally and globally (virtually) in their HQ in New York. During their Hispanic Heritage Month, I met Jorge Mina (president of the diversity council) who shared with me Henry's passion for Stanford. Jorge realized I had gone to Stanford too. I asked him to introduce me to Henry! I took the chance! To say I have cariño for Henry is an understatement. When we both first met over Zoom we connected over our love for learning new languages, traveling, foreign policy and diplomacy. I shared with him my Davos experiences and how I had traveled to forty countries.

It is no small achievement to be named one of thirty individuals chosen by *Barron's* to be the world's best CEOs—two different years straddling a global pandemic. Henry Fernandez, chairman and CEO of MSCI has done just that. As this is written he has logged two decades in that position, and the firm has revenues of more than $2.5 billion, and a market cap of $45 billion.

Henry could, in the generally accepted definition of the term, be characterized as "elite," but talking with him makes it very clear that he could not be further from "elitist." Born in Mexico, he moved (as a toddler) with his family to Nicaragua when his father was appointed to a diplomatic position. Despite his father's position, he remembers being shunned by those who considered themselves to be socially superior.

Then the family moved to the US and he began his undergraduate work, receiving a Bachelor of Arts in Economics at Georgetown University. That's when, as he phrases it, he became a "true global citizen." Immersed in foreign policy, he met people from all over the world, and "saw them adding perspectives I had not had before."

Having extended that education, first earning a Doctoral Studies in Economics at Princeton, and then getting a Master of Business Administration from Stanford, he landed on Wall Street, which he sees as a "complete meritocracy...what you do, what you produce is all that matters." When he was introduced as Cuban at one point, he was told "It doesn't matter."

And MSCI? He becomes almost elegiac: "I found one people, working for one cause, going in one direction, and attracting talent from all over."

During my interview with Henry, he taught me the value of family first. He taught me the principle of work-life balance. And how life, family and values are first. He shared an anecdote on when he had the opportunity to meet the King of Spain, however, that conflicted with a father-daughter trip he had planned ahead of time. He opted family first. He was right. Later in his career, he had the opportunity to meet the King of Spain. Destiny! Most importantly, family first. Many of us are caregivers, living with elderly parents, inclusion starts with I, who are you including and sponsoring?

Clearly, his is an experience that is living testimony to the *Return On Inclusion.*

Last but not least, a great principle I learned from Henry was gratitude. Giving back. He reminded me of my mom's advice: siempre lleva algo. Whenever someone treats you to lunch/dinner at their home, always bring a small thank you gift. Nominal value. It doesn't have to be expensive, just a token of gratitude. This small detail has gone a long way for me, as an immigrant entrepreneur, leader and CEO. Every year, a few weeks before Christmas, I have a Love Language Gifts Plan. I send thirty Merry Christmas letters with an alpaca hat made by the Peruvian women we empower at Pan Peru. I send it to my mentors, sponsors and friends who've opened their networks, who've introduced me to other leaders, and helped me in significant ways. Of course, Henry is part of this list. In addition to this, when I am introduced to another leader, I usually bring a small Peruvian gift like an alpaca scarf or Peruvian casino card games packet. People love gifts! Focus on being relational first. People remember how you made them feel. Thank you Henry!

MARIA FREIRE

I have to give credit to Jesus Mantas for connecting me with a true class act, Maria Freire. Jesus Mantas is a senior executive at IBM and board member of Biogen.

Perhaps there has never been a time in the contemporary age that global health has been more important than the years when the COVID pandemic replaced health and comfort with death and fear in country after country across the globe. The demands on healthcare leaders were severe. Their equanimity and expertise were crucial. As president and executive director of the Foundation for the National Institutes of Health from 2012 to 2021 (and also a member of the esteemed Council on Foreign Relations as well as the U.S. National Academy of Medicine), Maria Freire had a crucial role to play.

A native of Peru, she had completed her initial training there, before earning a PhD in biophysics at the University of Virginia then adding to that additional post-doctoral work at both the University of Tennessee and the Kennedy School of Government at Harvard. A series of increasingly responsible management roles in several not-for-profit organizations honed her skills and her interest in technology, medical intervention, biophysics and drug development. She was, to put it briefly, a "woman of the hour." She was keenly aware of how important innovation, aggressive but careful research, and the cross-fertilization of ideas would be, plus how central a role conscientious management would play for all three.

In terms of her personal goals, she is forthright:

> "In fact, that has always been one of my goals, that all the people who have worked with me, during all my years of career, can surpass me, be better people and professionals than I ever was or will be, and that is why I have always been one of the leaders who have supported new people and immigrants in the industry."

When I was interviewing Maria, I was struck by her boldness. She is a very firm and tough leader. As she explains it:

"My story is about a woman who had to reinvent herself...being Latina, woman, of being different, gave me the permission to look for paths that are not the traditional ones."

Evidently, we can see Maria embracing grit and tenacity in her career. Kudos to Maria for being a scientist, leader and public health official—something really hard to become, especially if you are a woman from Peru.

During our conversation with Maria, I agreed with her viewpoint—you can't be what you can't see. Maria is a firm believer in sponsorship. So am I. That's why Maria shared:

"It's very important to open the door to people who have all the capabilities but for some reason, whether it's their nationality, or gender, would not have been able to have them open."

TRICIA GELLMAN

Tricia and I met through Elias Torres. Elias Torres at the time was the co-founder and CTO of Drift. It was during the pandemic. We all met over Zoom and FaceTime. We bonded with Elias over our Christian values. Sometimes it's hard to find Christ-centered humans in tech. Elias and I shared Harvard affiliations, passion for Latin food, and diversity, but most importantly our faith. He connected me with his CMO: Tricia Gellman. Tricia and I bonded over walks in the north bay such as Tiburon and Sausalito.

Let's just say it up front: Tricia Gellman is hard to describe accurately without sounding breathless. Now she's advisor to the CEO and head of marketing at Tulip Interfaces, as well as advisor and mentor to the head of marketing at WorkRamp, plus a limited partner and advisor at Stage 2 Capital. When we did our interview, she was chief marketing officer at Drift. Before that, she worked her magic with some companies you may recognize:... Checkr...Apple...Adobe...Salesforce. And she steps beyond the standard corporate tasks to host a podcast and write a bi-monthly newsletter, all the while being careful to stay connected with her team. And, not surprisingly, she's straightforward about why. As she wrote in one newsletter: "...the only way to build a better culture is to be part of it. As a leader, that means making time to connect with your people."

She also pointed out that the larger teams grow, the easier it is to distance ourselves. When we asked her to suggest specific tactics to build a sense of belonging in the digital environment ushered in by COVID, she stepped right up.

Her first focus was on the importance of a level playing field. She stressed that a host of issues can crop up in a work-at-home world—different wifi speeds, dated equipment, limited access to appropriate workspace, children at home, etc.

And, she added, there are still some in the corporate world that have not yet caught on to the fact that building diversity and inclusion DO have data-driven positive effects on the bottom line, and thereby fail to recognize the power of collaboration.

GARY GUTHART

"In the CEO job, there are simply three things:

1. Is there a strategy for the organization to serve its mission and to prosper and can continue into the future?

2. Do you have the people in the organization and leadership who are aligned to your culture, who are outstanding leaders and can reflect the values of the org?

3. Do you have the operating processes, to get the work done?

Those are the three things.

Strategy gets a lot of business press. If you get the other two things right, it's key. EQ is strong. Is the org well led. From my perspective there are a whole of different personalities, what I am tracking: are people self motivated, do they have the courage of their convictions, there's more than ethics and truth, personal courage comes out in different ways, are you able to disagree, can you disagree without being totally abrasive? Interpersonal skills. Deeply competent. Deeply capable of what they're doing. They can speak truth to power. Top value is reality, describing the world how it is. You can't change the world if you don't know what the world is. What is the world?"

After spending nearly an hour, face to face with the CEO of Intuitive Surgical, a multi billion dollar health tech company, I learned the role of a CEO and how soft skills are as important as hard skills. He shares about finding value in people who are mature and emotionally smart enough to agree to disagree, to disagree without being abrasive or disrespectful. That's the key of true inclusion and belonging. Is bringing people together, people from diverse backgrounds, bringing unity, given that we live in such a polarized country, divided world, a world under several wars, we need to build a team with competent and interpersonal skills people. People who can speak truth to power by not being arrogant, but by being respectful and servant leadership.

Gary said:

"There's a line in the poem if you can dream but don't let your dream be your master."

I think that the idea that you need to be able to dream but not be possessed by your dreams. This idea of where are we really now. You have to be grounded in reality. At the same time have the vision for the future and be able and willing to pursue it. That balance I think is super important in people. Part of that assessment is can people do both."

Personal courage. Being able to disagree, by not being disagreeable.

When you turn 18 in the United States
nobody expects you to stay home.
You go to college; you go to boarding
and once that is done you never get to
live back to your home. If you do get
back people see you as a failure.
In the United States, you have to
prove yourself and get lucky,
that's a big differentiator.

~ Alejandro Valenzuela | CEO of Banco Azteca

ENDNOTES

1   https://www.bostonglobe.com/2022/02/22/opinion/ibm-e-mails-about-making-dinobabies-extinct-confirm-what-older-workers-already-know/

2   https://www.ibm.com/impact/be-equal/

3   https://hbr.org/big-ideas

4   Gerhardt, Megan W., Josephine Nachemson-Ekwall, and Brandon Fogel. Gentelligence the Revolutionary Approach to Leading an Intergenerational Workforce. Lanham: Rowman & Littlefield, 2021

5   https://www.channelfutures.com/business-models/dell-technologies-world-the-best-of-michael-dells-keynote

CHAPTER FOUR

Gender Front and Center

—

Among those working—in whatever role—within the DEI arena, the discussion of the "progress" regarding women in the workplace is lively. It typically involves one of two points of view—which are more different than they are alike:

1. Much of the energy and activity in the field focuses on women, certainly more than any of the other affected groups.

2. Yes, some progress has been made, but bias persists. Perhaps there is more diversity, but equity and inclusion still need work. Even with diversity, some of the measurement is off the mark.

The amount of literature on this subject is massive. Not only is there lack of consensus, but many of the authors are women who can write not only about what they've witnessed, but what they've experienced.

And the public interest and attention to the subject of gender as a whole rose exponentially with the leak in early May 2022 of a US Supreme Court document that seemed to indicate the Roe v Wade decision regarding abortion might be struck down, which of course it eventually was.

Let's take a look at the corporate status quo.

Typically, the complaint about the closing of the gender gap focuses on measurements that simply count the number/percentage of females in the ranks, without sufficient attention to whether they are in positions of increasing responsibility and influence. Most importantly, it is not just about the number of women in the organization, but what percentage of women have a mentor? What percentage of women have a sponsor? How many women were promoted within the last year? In comparison to males? Retention rates? Promotion rates? Churn rates? In a March 2022 summary of research findings, Dagny Dukach, associate editor at *Harvard Business Review,* goes a step further and catalogs what changes ensue—if any—when women join the C-suite ranks. Three examples:

- There can be an impact on the overall corporate culture, as evidenced by a drop in gender-stereotyped language.

- Not only do women earn less than their male counterparts, but those in top management teams earn less if they work for a female CEO than they do working for a male CEO.

- When there are ethical problems, female leaders who openly object face more retaliation than do men.

Also, in March 2022 in the *Harvard Business Review,* three university professors discussed how gender bias persists even in female-dominated industries, such as law, higher education, healthcare and faith-based not-for-profit organizations. Among the problems reported by female participants were:

- The need to downplay their achievements.

- Lack of acknowledgment of their contributions.

- Men interrupting while they were speaking.

- Exclusion and workplace harassment.

- Lack of support for combining work and family obligations.

At this writing, the jury is still out on the final effect the COVID pandemic will have on the US business world. It assuredly, though, has thrown the spotlight on a raft of inequities, not the least of which is the wage gap between men and women. As part of the Brookings Institution Gender Equality series, authors Nicole Bateman and Martha Ross marshalled several telling statistics,[1] including:

- Of the women working in low-paying jobs, 15% are single parents and 41% live in households with incomes below 200% of the federal poverty level, which the authors estimate to be roughly $43,000 for a family of three.

- The majority of women between the ages of 18 and 64 work, and one in four of them have a child under 14 at home.

- Between February and April 2020, the unemployment rate for women increased by 12 percentage points compared to less than 10 percentage points for men. Or, to put it another way, between February and August, mothers of children up to the age of 12 lost 2.2 million jobs, compared to 870,000 for men.

Noting that while COVID issues have exacerbated the challenges facing women in the workplace, the authors stress that since many of the conditions are longstanding, the solutions must be more than temporary. To wit:

Other policies that could increase women's labor force participation, close the wage gap, and make work more accessible for mothers include policies that incentivize or fund predictable work scheduling, guaranteed number of work hours, and extended school-day or before and after school programs. We are long overdue in realigning our labor market policies, schools, and daycare system with the modern reality faced by working parents; these interventions should be considered as part of the solution.

The already-complicated issues surrounding gender have escalated now to encompass the focus on an individuals ability to choose which gender they prefer.

Currently serving as Chief Legal Officer and corporate secretary at Seagen, Jean Liu has more than two decades' experience in the biotech industry, much of it spent working as general counsel.

Her perspective on inclusion, specifically but not only as it relates to women, is informed not only by her own experience but also by what she has witnessed in recent years. Quite prevalent, she says, is "availability bias," defining it in simple terms as "what you see is all that you know." Because of that, companies interested in promoting diversity and inclusion tend to pull from a limited list of candidates because the existing decision makers continue to be predominately white males who live in the same zip codes, belong to the same clubs, etc., and therefore are part of limited networks. Recalling her own experience, she suggested that for those seeking new challenges or positions, it is important to "tell people what you want to do."

Finally, while we're on the subject of gender, it may come as a surprise to many readers that the idea of more than two genders is by no means new. An episode of the PBS show "Independent Lens" that aired in August 2015 includes the following in its online script:

On nearly every continent, and for all recorded history, thriving cultures have recognized, revered, and integrated more than two genders. Terms such as "transgender" and "gay" are strictly new constructs that assume three things: that there are only two sexes (male/female), as many as two sexualities (gay/straight), and only two genders (man/woman).

Yet hundreds of distinct societies around the globe have their own long-established traditions for third, fourth, fifth, or more genders.

The text continues by presenting as examples the Navajo nádleehí, one child who is both a boy and a girl and the Hawaiian mahu, embodying both male and female spirits.[2]

Our own Peruvian indigenous culture is one of several in North and South America who give credence to the prophecy of "The Eagle and the Condor," essentially balance between the former, representing male energy—the predominance of the mind... science...technology, sometimes articulated as darkness and the latter, female energy—the predominance of the heart and rendered as lightness. The ideal, remember, is balance.

Maria has spent most of her career at Fortune 10 companies and having been a C-level executive herself, she shares her perspective on women in the workplace in two dimensions.

1. It's time to give women the stretch roles. She has seen firsthand how much coaching and mentoring goes on with women and she believes the best teacher is experience, so give women the roles, give them the coaching and mentoring as she delivers, and allow for women to continue to rise in the workplace through their increasing competency.

2. Acknowledgment that there is still room for improvement in how we talk about women in the workplace. Being

mindful that we use the same descriptors of behavior in men and women leaders is a great start. The next time you catch yourself saying "She's aggressive," challenge yourself to think how you would describe that same behavior in a man.

Maria shared that one of the best examples she saw of real-time leadership was when she was chief of staff to the CEO of a business unit, when participating in a succession planning meeting with the Executive Leadership Team she witnessed an officer describe a woman as having "sharp elbows." The CEO of the group in a humble way asked the officer, "I wonder, would we say the same if she was a he?" and by that simple question, in which the CEO made himself part of the problem—he *included* himself in the question—the CEO made the remark non-threatening and gave the officer the space he needed to rethink and reframe his comment. It completely changed the tone of the rest of the discussion.

In another example, when Maria was in a succession planning discussion as a board member, she saw a very innocent conversation turn into a great learning experience for the table. In this instance, the discussion was around a female leader who would be promoted to a senior executive role. Every director knew this leader—a clear nod to her competency and excellence in her current role—and was supportive of the move. However, a couple of the directors also knew she was going through a personal hardship and made a comment to the CEO to ensure that they were properly supporting her and that the promotion didn't become something she couldn't do. Please understand that the comment was born out of true care for the individual, and with all the best of intentions, but this is where we all have a need to be aware of the framing of our thoughts and their appropriateness to the discussion. In this case, it was another director—who happened to be the DEI officer of another company—who chimed in and said gently but firmly, "we should trust our leaders to accept whatever challenge they can handle or not." It was a brilliant statement. Notice that she didn't make any of us feel bad for the conversation. She didn't admonish the comment, she didn't even ask us to compare our thoughts based on gender. Instead, she just stated a fact that reminded us at that table that even with the best of intentions and with the most innocent of reasons, we could slip into non-inclusive moments.

So again, be aware of how you think of women in the workplace. Are you coaching them because they still need more development or because you care too much and don't want them to fail? And are you looking at male and female leaders through the same business lens?

And for the women reading this book, Maria has a request that if you've heard her speak to crowds before on this subject, you knew it was coming. She says, "the next time someone comes to you to speak negatively or critically about a woman, please reply with 'so how do we help her.'" And if we want to change the conversation around women in business, let's start with each other. Her challenge is for all women to support each other in the workplace through complements of competency like "love how you handled that meeting" or "nice job on a project delivered early and under budget."

The struggle is real. The juggle is real. This is why everyone should hire working mothers. They are put in crazy situations all the time and are forced to problem-solve. They are some of my most resourceful employees.

~ Sara Blakeley | Founder of Spanx

PERSPECTIVES ON POINT

Insights Gained From Personal Interviews by the Authors

CARLOS GUTIERREZ

Carlos and I met through the power of the Berkeley network. As a passionate super-connector, I have the habit of catching up every quarter with meaningful relationships such as:

1. Alumni from Berkeley, Stanford, and Harvard.
2. Friends from the World Economic Forum (Shapers, Young Global Leaders, WEF Technology Pioneers, WEF Social Innovators and fellow 1t.org board members).
3. Fellow creators from the LinkedIn Creator Accelerator Program.
4. Fellow delegates, friends and listers from the Forbes 30 Under 30 Summit.
5. Fellow awardees from the NextGen 30 Under 30 list presented by Goldman Sachs.

As you can see, many of these connections live in major metropolitan cities such as San Francisco, London, New York, Melbourne, Bangkok, Singapore, Doha, Dubai, Lima, Sao Paulo, etc., so whenever I travel I am intentional in reaching out. Anyway, when I was in the south bay near Los Gatos, I reached out to my good friend and mentor John Cleveland. John and I met through the SkyDeck Accelerator program when I was a first-time tech founder. I was presiding over SmileyGo, 19 years old when I founded it at Stanford, and my startup got into Berkeley SkyDeck. SkyDeck offered a variety of solid mentors, at the time, John Cleveland was the CHRO of Seagate. John and I bonded over our passion for startups, how we enjoy teaching (he teaches at SJSU and I used to teach entrepreneurship at Tecnologico de Monterrey), our love for Pepperdine, and our bonds with Parkinson's: my mother has Parkinson's and so did his father-in-law. Periodically, John and I would grab a meal in Los Gatos, after I graduated from Berkeley. During one of our get-togethers, we were talking about angel investing and startups when John mentioned Empath: Empath provides clients with a highly accurate company-wide skills inventory that includes skill proficiency levels by employee and by job role. Skills are matched to current and future roles, as well as to training and course-work. Our insights into a company's skills portfolio enable a skills-based approach to talent management. This AI startup seemed really cool, given my expertise on the future of work, I wanted to meet the CEO! Turns out, former Secretary of Commerce and Kellogg's CEO—Carlos Gutierrez—was the co-founder and CEO of Empath. John made the warm email introduction (my favorite type of emails) and boom, we hit it off. Carlos and I bonded over our Judeo-Christian values, passion for traveling and public speaking. It is truly thanks to him that I'm part of the speaking bureau: Leading Authorities. He opened so many doors for me as a technology investor, AI entrepreneur, published author and keynote speaker. Growing up in Peru, I would visit Miami twice a year to stay with my extended family. South Florida is known for its delicious Cuban food such as La Carreta and the tasty Pollo Tropical chains. I shared with Carlos my love for Cuban food—we bonded. He likes Peruvian cuisine too. During our initial conversations we talked about our family backgrounds: I shared with him how my grandmother Julia started everything in the Peruvian Amazon rainforest—the restaurant, gas station and trucking business with my grandfather Pedro. He shared how his father had a pineapple business. We bonded over our family business backgrounds. Later throughout our friendship, we met in person to grab lunch at The Ritz-Carlton Georgetown in Washington, DC. I shared with him how I gave a TED Talk Build The Bridge at Georgetown in 2017. Small world. Lessons I learned from Carlos was to always stay in touch with your friends, connections and acquaintances, never burn bridges, and be intentional in building your network from scratch. By the way, he was the youngest CEO of Kellogg's in history. Wow! Kudos to you Carlos!

"The responsibility for trust is in the
senior leadership. The higher you
go, the more responsible you are
for trust.... Leaders have to prove to
employees that they can be trusted."

No doubt about this. I agree with Carlos on the trust topic.
Leaders are held accountable, and need to be held accountable for
their work, trust is crucial. My dad would always mention "One
who is faithful in a very little is also faithful in much, and one who
is dishonest in a very little is also dishonest in much." which is Luke
16:10. Trust is an essential trait of a leader.

"Anything that makes someone
different than the group,
someone that makes someone
part of the other, will always make
them feel like outsiders. And the
big challenge is for people, number
one, to recognize that they feel like
outsiders. And number two, to have
enough empathy to make them feel
like they're part of the group."

Empathy is so important these days. Carlos is spot on when he talks about embracing empathy in all circumstances. This reminds me of the Empathy keynote I gave at T-Mobile for their engineering and sales teams. Especially for the non-product people (who usually don't think about user interface, user experience, product workflow), I focused the workshop on the importance of having the empathy DNA to make outsiders feel a sense of belonging. Bring your whole self to work.

> ## "We're beginning to realize that the scope of diversity is not as narrow as we thought. Anything that makes people feel like the other should be included."

Yes to being included! We need to be intentional when it comes to making people feel included, 100% agreed with Carlos. This reminds me of the wonderful lunch we had together at the Ritz Carlton in Georgetown. If we truly want people to bring their whole selves to work we must be intentional in having an open dialogue.

Public sector, private sector...managing, consulting...products, people...Carlos Gutierrez has been there, done that:

Public: US Secretary of Commerce during the George W. Bush Administration.

Private: President and CEO of the Kellogg Company (at that time, the only Latin CEO of a Fortune 500 company.

Managing: In 2004, *Fortune* magazine called him "the man who fixed Kellogg."

Consulting: Founder and chairman of *Global Political Strategies*

Products: In the late 20th century, when Kellogg faced decreasing cereal sales, he saved the day with his "Volume to Value" plan focusing resources on higher-margin products.

People: At this writing, chairman and CEO of Empath, a firm that provides machine learning technology to improve how talent is managed in large organizations thereby boosting performance and retention.

And then there are multiple appointments to boards of directors of major firms.

Drawing from both the breadth and depth of his experience, and with the kind of honesty and candor that is his trademark, Carlos "cut to the chase" in our interview.

Whom should we "include" when we address the inclusion issue? Anything, he says, that makes someone "feel part of the other," will keep them from feeling part of the group, so inclusion stretches further than the typical categories of gender, race, culture, etc.

How are we doing statistically? Unfortunately, in his opinion, companies have been taught to turn to an increase in hiring of members of affected as "proof." This approach fails to provide a comprehensive solution to the problem at hand. While increased representation is essential, it barely scratches the surface of the multifaceted issue of diversity and inclusion within corporate environments.

Beyond the mere numerical representation of diverse groups, there exist vital yet frequently overlooked metrics that truly gauge the inclusivity and equity within a workplace. Factors such as turnover rates among minority groups, the perceived value employees place on their work, and the extent to which they feel genuinely valued by the organization are crucial aspects that often get sidelined in the pursuit of numerical diversity targets.

The true measure of an inclusive and progressive corporate culture lies not just in the numbers but in the qualitative aspects of employee experiences. It's about fostering an environment where individuals from diverse backgrounds thrive, where their skills are not just recognized but continuously honed and valued. When employees feel supported, appreciated, and offered opportunities for growth, it not only boosts morale but also creates an inclusive corporate culture.

And how can we improve the element of trust in the workplace? In many ways, business is like politics. The higher on the leadership scale one operates, the more responsibility they have for creating an environment that feels safe and encourages a two-way flow of ideas.

In March 2022, American Compass published a quote that crisply describes Carlos' overall point of view regarding potential for the US corporate and political worlds:

> We can give the world confidence that openness works. That openness creates jobs. That openness creates prosperity and openness leads to better lives in China and in the U.S. And, I believe the world would like to hear that message from us.[3]

BILL HAWKINS

Having served as CEO of both Medtronics and Immucor, Bill Hawkins continues to plumb his comprehensive experience in the healthcare arena by having served on the Duke University Board of Trustees, as well as chair of the board of university's healthcare system. He also is senior advisor to EW Healthcare Partners, headquartered in New York. Both he and Greg Buchert (see page 43) are advisors to Pluto Healthcare a staffing operation that recruits and places traveling nurses, an operation that Hawkins describes as "transformational."

Recalling his management team at Medtronics, Bill points out that, yes, indeed the group was diverse, but not because the individuals were chosen based on their race or gender or age, etc., but because of their experience and demonstrated skills. "When we talk about diversity and inclusion," he explained, "it's important to move beyond the 'optics,' and deal with issues such as intellect, background, and performance."

It is important to note that Bill's perspective on the inclusion issue derives from an experience base jam-packed with service on boards of directors as well as in management and operations and is not restricted to the United States. The final two paragraphs of his profile on the Duke University Board of Trustees website give you an idea:

He is a Senior Advisor to EW Healthcare Partners, a leading private equity firm investing in life sciences. He is Chairman of the Board of Bioventus (BVS:Nasdaq) and on the Board of Virtue Labs, Baebies, Cereius, Cirtec Medical, Biogen (BIIB: NASDAQ), MiMedX (NASDAQ: MDXG) and lead director of Immucor. He is on the Global Advisory Board of Home Instead, Senior Care. Mr. Hawkins is the past Chairman and Co-Founder of the Medical Device Innovation Consortium ("MDIC") and past president of the American Institute of Medical and Biological Engineering ("AMIBE"). Mr. Hawkins was elected to the Duke University Board of Trustees in 2011 and currently serves on the Executive Committee, Audit and Compliance Committee, and External Engagement Committee. Mr. Hawkins is Chair of the Board of the Duke University Health System. He is a member of the NC Biotech board and serves on the Board of the Focused Ultrasound Foundation Society.

Mr. Hawkins also serves as a Member of the Advisory Boards at Arboretum Ventures, Hatteras Venture Partners, HealthQuest Ventures, and past member of A*STAR SERC Cluster Advisory Board in Singapore, and the Biomedical Research Council of Singapore.[4]

JOHN HENNESSY

Words are not enough to describe my utmost joy when I think of John Hennessy. Why joy? Bill Coleman (founder of BEA Systems) connected me with John in 2020. Bill, was such a dear mentor and friend of mine. We used to grab breakfast every month at Rick's Cafe in Los Altos, CA. Bill opened so many doors in my career by connecting me with Eric Schmidt, Doug Merritt and Dan Schulman for my first book: *Differences That Make a Difference.* When John and I met, during COVID, we had a Zoom conversation. I shared with him my love for Stanford and how it changed my life: coming from the very competitive environment at Berkeley to a collaborative ecosystem at Stanford, that enabled me to grow as a Type A, hyper-joyful entrepreneur and driven founder. We bonded over our mutual friends with John, such as my co-author Jorge Titinger and others.

> ## "There's a lot of progress that's being made, but it's going to take a long time to grapple with how we're going to mitigate or eliminate built-in inequalities that get built into our system very early on."

Talking about Stanford reminds me of the interview I led with John Hennessy, the Chairman of Alphabet Inc. For those who don't know, Alphabet owns Google, Waymo and other behemoths. In addition, John served as the President of Stanford from 2010 to 2018. Our good friend Bill Coleman (CEO of Veritas) put us in touch. I agree with John that there is a lot of work to be done given the inequalities that were created in the past, for both Hispanics and Blacks. Why are Hispanics forgotten? Good question. While we are 20% of the country's population you see less Hispanic board members than other ethnic/cultural groups such as Black and/or Asians.

In a January 2021 episode of the podcast #ThePlaybook, John described what he calls "the formula" for building great companies by detailing three components:

1. A culture of empathy and emotional intelligence.

2. An acknowledgment and understanding that the focus is "about doing great things for your customers and for your employees. It's not just about trying to make yourself fantastically rich before you're 40."

3. Assurance that every employee is a stockholder.

When we asked him to describe what he expects in the next few years in terms of "virtual work" plans, he describes a hybrid environment, because people naturally "crave interaction." He is quick to add that successful teamwork depends on a recognition that teams formed before the pandemic and now working virtually are quite different from those formed as virtual teams.

Central to John's success as a leader in both academic and corporate arenas is a firm sense of values. The first chapter of his book *Leading Matters: Lessons from My Journey* is titled "Humility: the Basis for Effective Leadership." It begins this way:

> Most people, looking from the outside, assume that *confidence* is the heart of leadership.... No one wants to follow a leader who seems unsure of his plans or her own abilities. What lies at the heart of confidence?
>
> I happen to think that real confidence—that is, not a mask of confidence, or phony bravado, or worst of all, misplaced confidence, but a true sense of one's own skills and character—arises not from ego, but from humility.

Arrogance sees only our strengths, ignores our weaknesses, and overlooks the strengths of others, therefore leaving us vulnerable to catastrophic mistakes. Humility shows us where our weaknesses lie so we can compensate for them. Humility makes us earn our confidence.

Makes sense—and also makes you want to read more. We did. It's rich—in the very best sense of that word.

RODRIGO LIANG

Rodrigo and I were introduced by a wonderful human: Ana Pinczuk. Ana, originally from Argentina, is a dear friend of mine who loves real football: soccer. From meeting in Qatar for the 2022 World Cup to grabbing lunch in Burlingame, California, we share the same core family values of giving back and dreaming. Ana serves on the board of trustees at Cornell University and other major companies. She connected me with Rodrigo, given that he was raised in Brazil and is also an AI founder. Rodrigo and I bonded immediately, after I mentioned how my cousin married a Brazilian woman from Minas Gerais: we started talking a bit in Portuguese! I love Brazilian food such as fejoada, caju, farinha and picanha. We bonded over Brazilian churrasqueria. It's truly impressive to see how South American immigrants are crushing it in Silicon Valley. Born in Taiwan and raised in Brazil, Rodrigo is a perfect example of diversity of background. Parabens Rodrigo!

"We're going fast, we have a responsibility to play our share, right?

We have our piece to help the world transition, and we got to do our share and other people have to do their share as well. And if you do it right, then we're being a better place."

I can't agree more with Rodrigo Liang, my great Brazilian friend. All of us have to do our part in order to get the return on inclusion. Even if you are a startup, you don't need a chief inclusion officer but you do need to start since day one. What is your goal? What is your strategy? Who are you sponsoring? Who are you vouching for?

"Great people bring great people. Businesses about relationships and how you connect with people."

Wise words from Rodrigo, one of the few Latin founders in Silicon Valley to have a unicorn valuation for his AI startup.

"You build,
you provide value to people.
And if you do that,
you have a business."

I would always remember my Stanford engineering classes, where my professor Tom Kosnik said: if you solve a problem for 1 million people, you'll be a millionaire. If you solve a need for 1 billion people, you'll be a billionaire. Rodrigo also went to Stanford. Let's go Cardinals!

If you're not careful, visiting the SambaNova System website can make you feel a little breathless. Or, alternatively, if you're a gym rat, you'll have to settle for excited. It's all about what's happening and how fast. Among the factoids, are these two:

1. 63% of CEOs believe that AI will have a larger impact than the Internet.

2. AI will add $50 trillion to the economy in the next decade.

SambaNova Systems is the third start-up for Rodrigo Liang, and while he tells us they're all different, that doesn't make him any less excited. In an October 2021 interview with IEEE Spectrum, he was asked for an example that adequately captures the potential for what—hardware and software—the firm provides. His answer was a partnership with Argonne National Laboratories to map the Universe. "Map the Universe, can you imagine that?"[5]

Despite the fact that his company and the services it provides are a mélange of high-end technology, Rodrigo is quick to insist that like any other business, it is in the end "about relationships and how you connect with people." His own background gives him an up close and personal idea about how seriously those in leadership roles in the US need to pay attention to cultural norms. His family is originally from Taiwan, and he grew up in Brazil, and went to a German school, coming to this country as a teenager. He speaks Chinese, Portuguese, and English, and apologizes because his Spanish isn't better. Multi-culturism matters, he insists, a lot. After meeting him a handful of times both virtually and in his Palo Alto office, I've learnt Rodrigo's passion for cultural intelligence and how that has helped him become a better leader. The best ideas come from diverse teams.

JEAN LIU

Jean and I met through Marc Tarpenning (cofounder of Tesla) in 2018. Marc was a guest speaker at Berkeley, he is also an alumn, and after his speech I chased him. We became friends and he helped me with my first book: *Differences That Make a Difference.*

Currently serving as Chief Legal Officer and corporate secretary at Seagen, Jean Liu has more than two decades experience in the biotech industry, much of it spent working as general counsel. In addition to being an outstanding C-suite executive and lawyer, she serves on the board of directors of Erasca, Connect Biopharma and Angarus Therapeutics. Her perspective on inclusion, specifically but not only as it relates to women, is informed not only by her own experience by what she has witnessed in recent years.

Quite prevalent, she says,
is "availability bias," defining it
in simple terms as "what you
see is all that you know."
Because of that, companies interested
in promoting diversity and inclusion
tend to pull from a limited list of
candidates because the existing
decision makers continue to be
predominately white males who
live in the same zip codes, belong to
the same clubs, etc., and therefore
are part of limited networks.

Recalling her own experience, she suggested that for those seeking new challenges or positions, it is important to "tell people what you want to do."

At the point in her own career that she wished to expand her board experience to both private and public companies, she simply mentioned that desire to a long-term peer and friend. When he took over as CEO and was building his own list of board candidates, he remembered that exchange, and happily added her name.

Liu's natural bent for looking for solutions and focusing on the agreed-upon goals for a given project or within the corporate culture clearly is a driver in many situations. As she put it in a 2016 interview: "I really enjoy being at the crossroads of business, science, and the law while exercising different skills and expertise. But I still look forward to discovering new challenges and passions where I can apply myself in fresh ways."[6]

SHELLYE ARCHAMBEAU

Shellye and I not only talked about inclusion but also on risk-taking, and the importance that has when it comes to failing forward. Here is what Shellye shared in regards to taking risks:

> "Risk and opportunity are two sides of the same coin. So if you're not taking risks, then you're not going to get the opportunities."

I 100% agree with Shellye. I wouldn't be where I am today, if I didn't take risks. I took a risk to drop out of the Full IB program in high school. I took a risk in dropping out of an academic term at Stanford to fully focus on my fintech startup SmileyGo. I took a risk in moving to the U.S. at the age of 18 to pursue higher education at Berkeley, leaving my parents' home in Peru. I'm thankful God opened doors, opportunities for me to excel in. Risk and opportunity are two sides of the same coin, indeed, you're so right Shellye. Later, in our conversation, Shellye explained what it means to take risks by sharing:

"Taking risks means putting yourself in a position in which you feel uncomfortable...that discomfort is all part of taking risks that are part of personally growing."

This reminded me of my early days in Silicon Valley. Was it uncomfortable to take multivariable classes at Stanford? Was it hard to enroll in computer science classes? was it challenging to create a tech startup while pursuing my bachelor of science degree? Heck yes. But, it was worth it. I learned to operate on my edge.

Last but not least, we talked about failure—Shellye shared "you're only defined by failure if you don't learn from it and move forward because once you learn from it, move forward, then it's just a learning exercise." Failing forward is a muscle, same as creativity. Let's learn from our past mistakes and move forward. Let's push code, deploy, iterate, learn, lets go—VAMOS!

ENDNOTES

1 https://www.brookings.edu/articles/why-has-covid-19-been-especially-harmful-for-working-women/

2 https://www.pbs.org/independentlens/content/two-spirits_map-html

3 https://americancompass.org/quote/charity-1-carlos-m-gutierrez/

4 https://trustees.duke.edu/william-hawkins-iii-e76/

5 https://spectrum.ieee.org/sambanova-ceo-ai-interview

6 https://www.linkedin.com/in/jeaniliu

CHAPTER FIVE

Remotely Speaking

—

> In the middle of difficulty,
> lies opportunity.
>
> ~ Albert Einstein

The disruption in both economic and social arenas caused by COVID has yet to be adequately measured, but the prevailing opinion at this writing is that in most countries, and almost certainly in the United States, we cannot assume we will return to pre-pandemic norms.

Already we have witnessed what was originally dubbed "The Great Resignation." In a survey conducted by the Pew Research Center in early 2022, the three reasons participants cited for their decisions to resign in 2021 were low pay, no opportunity for advancement, and feeling disrespected, in that order. Number four was child-care issues.

So, did they swell the unemployment ranks? Hardly. Not counting those who reported having retired, the majority said they were employed—55% full-time and 23% part-time. Difficult to find a job? Six in ten said no. Even more telling:

> For the most part, workers who quit a job last year and are now employed somewhere else see their current work situation as an improvement over their most recent job. At least half of these workers say that compared with their last job, they are now earning more money (56%), have more opportunities for advancement (53%), have an easier time balancing work and family responsibilities (53%) and have more flexibility to choose when they put in their work hours (50%).

> Still, sizable shares say things are either worse or unchanged in these areas compared with their last job. Fewer than half of workers who quit a job last year (42%) say they now have better benefits, such as health insurance and paid time off, while a similar share (36%) says it's about the same. About one-in-five (22%) now say their current benefits are *worse* than at their last job.[1]

Some analysts, writers and human resource specialists find it especially telling that a drop in benefits is tolerable especially at a time when healthcare coverage for family members can hover around $1,000 per month per person.

A McKinsey survey in April 2021 found employers planning a hybrid virtual model after the pandemic, in part to capture and perpetuate the increase in productivity they've experienced but warned that those employers who fail to address employee reports of anxiety and burnout may find the productivity increases unsustainable. As the authors put it "because anxiety is known to reduce job satisfaction, negatively affect interpersonal relationships with colleagues, and decrease work performance." The source of the anxiety? Employees don't know the specifics of their employers' plans.[2]

Does that bellow "inclusion" or what?

Employers' enthusiasm has been anything but overwhelming, however. In a July 2021 *New York Times* article written by Austan Goolsbee, a professor of economics at the University of Chicago Booth School of Business, Goldman Sachs CEO David Solomon was quoted as describing remote work as an "aberration," with Morgan Stanley CEO James Gorman taking a firm stand as well: "If you want to get paid New York rates, you work in New York."[3]

Gorman's position introduces what many analysts believe is the core issue regarding pandemic-born changes in business practice: a breakdown of trust between business leaders and employees. In fact, indications are, the schism affects not just employees, but investors, customers, etc.

That's the great irony of allowing passionate people to work from home. A manager's natural instinct is to worry that her workers aren't getting enough work done. But the real threat is that they will wind up working too hard.

~ Jason Fried

PERSPECTIVES ON POINT

Insights Gained From Personal Interviews by the Authors

TSU-JAE KING LIU

In effecting change—be it in science, in business or in professional/personal relationships—one can do, be, model, innovate, lead, manage, or execute. (Not an exhaustive list, but at least a foundation.) Dr. Tsu-Jae King Liu is about as good an example as one might find of how to make that happen. Briefly:

> The first woman to hold the position of dean of the College of Engineering at the University of California, Berkeley. In that role, she: has bolstered efforts to recruit outstanding new faculty members who value diversity, equity and inclusion, and to enhance the success and well-being of all engineering students at Berkeley. She aims to effect a cultural transformation within the college—and within the field of engineering in general—to be more welcoming, inclusive and socially connected, to help ensure that engineering innovations have broad, positive impact with minimal unintended negative consequences."[4]

Holder of more than ninety US patents, one of them for a transistor design used in all leading-edge microprocessor chips.

A member of the board of directors of Intel and MaxLinear.

A member of the US National Academy of Engineering.

This is why I love writing books. I get to know these outstanding leaders, Fortune 500 CEOs and board members. I get to know these humans by not only interviewing them, but by breaking bread, playing tennis, pickleball, soccer, basketball, golf and hikes. Tsu-Jae is a person I admire, by her core values and commitment to inclusion.

Tsu-Jae and I met through Carol Christ, the Chancellor of Berkeley. The best public university in the world, my Alma Mater. When we met, we both found out we had mutual friends such as Pat Gelsinger (Intel CEO). Tsu-Jae, in addition to being the first woman to be the Dean of Berkeley Engineering, served on the board of directors at Intel. I shared with Tsu-Jae how I attended Peninsula Covenant Church in Redwood City—a church Pat has attended in the past. Small world! We shared the same core value of generosity, giving back to our community, joy, and thankfulness. We started a long-lasting friendship. Since our first interview, Tsu-Jae has supported Pan Peru by purchasing the handmade alpaca hats created by the women entrepreneurs we support in the Andes. When we talked about the data behind inclusion, Tsu-Jae expressed:

> "The data is pretty clear. Companies that have more diversity in their leadership and board of directors generally perform better—they're in the upper quartile of business performance metrics."

Certainly, I agree with Tsu-Jae. The data is clear. Numbers speak for themselves. Nevertheless, in this specific topic it is necessary for us—business leaders—to share and pronounce the numbers out loud. Further in our conversation, Tsu-Jae shared about our responsibility as STEM leaders:

> "As engineers and scientists, we should face the data that's collected properly; the facts will tell you if there's an issue, and if there is, then at least you can think of ways to find out what the root causes are and test out solutions."

That's the beauty of numbers, math and science—it's purely objective. We can test and iterate new solutions. The Silicon Valley way of shipping products, testing, launching and deploying. Last but not least, Tsu-Jae shared:

> ## "Investing in diversity is not just about numbers; it's about ensuring inclusion and belonging. If people's voices aren't heard, what's the point?"

Golden nuggets at their best!

MONICA LOZANO

The way I met Monica was a unique one. I met her through my Berkeley connections which started in 2013. As many know, the first nine college letters were rejection letters. Berkeley was the last one to notify me. My dad encouraged me to pray. Berkeley accepted me with merit-based scholarships. During the CAA Leadership Award Scholarships luncheon, the executive director Jefferson Coombs asked for a guest speaker. 300 student leaders in the room. No one raised their hands. I took the risk, mom would tell me to have faith and go for it. I gave a three minute speech on how thankful I am towards the donors for the scholarships. Rosemary Mein was one of the donors, she approached me after my speech congratulating me for my joy and energy. Next thing I know, we are golfing together in Orinda. Through the Berkeley network I got introduced to Michael Torres, CEO of Adelante Capital who connected me with Luis Orozco. Luis graciously introduced me to Monica Lozano while I was the Vice President of business development at the Silicon Valley Leadership Group.

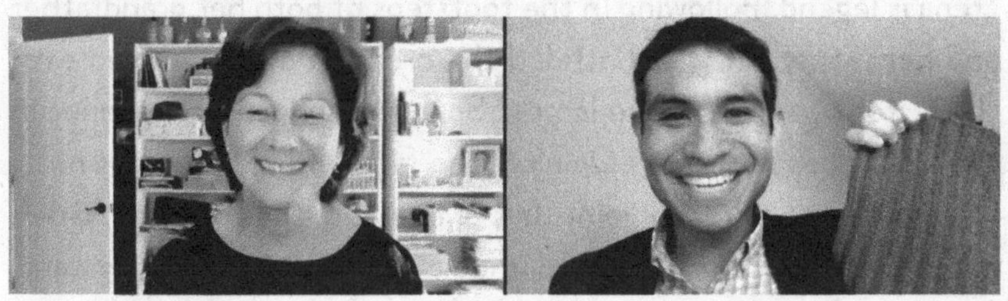

During my conversation with Monica Lozano, we talked about the complexities of being a first-generation immigrant, woman or minority trying to understand the US economy and how to break the ceiling:

> ## "Very often, the thing that keeps you back is you don't know how to navigate the system."

And this is so true! In the beginning, when you are new in this country, English is not your mother tongue, it is hard to navigate the entire system. I remember the first few times I sat in a Stanford Engineering classroom, Berkeley Haas classroom, and many of my classmates said "oh yeah Pedro, my aunt works at VMware, my dad is at Cisco, my mom is at Nvidia, and my uncle works at Meta." And then, there was me! International student, immigrant from

Peru, who had zero network in Silicon Valley. But this INSPIRED me to build my network from scratch. This fueled my motivation to create meaningful relationships over time by focusing on being relational over transactional.

Monica Lozano's leadership—and success—in the print media arena is legend. Following in the footsteps of both her grandfather and her father, she has both led the creation of and moved with the historic growth of the largest Spanish-language newspaper in the US. It began with *La Opinion*, the family newspaper business. Recognizing at a critical point that to compete the company had to extend its reach into the multi-media world, she pushed forward. She now chairs the board of US Hispanic Media, Inc., the parent company of ImpreMediaLLC, which today owns La Opinion, plus a good number of the other major regional Hispanic newspapers, online media outlets, etc.

Monica's leadership roles have included board seats—University of California Regents (Chair) Apple, Target Corporation, Bank of America, Walt Disney Company and the Weingart (Chair) and Rockefeller Foundations—and participation on state (California Commission on the 21st Century Economy) and national (President Obama's Economic Recovery Advisory Board, which became the President's Council on Jobs and Competitiveness) levels. In 2014, when the Aspen Institute solicited her help in putting together its Latinos and Society Program, she put together an advisory board that crossed sectoral and ethnic divides and assumed her position as chair. She was appointed to the Apple Inc. board of directors in January 2021.

As she reflects on the growth of her business(es), Lozano attributes the trajectory to the development of quality content designed to "inform, educate and empower the community." She emphasizes this was not "transactional," but instead focused on lasting relationships. As you know, we too believe relationships are at the heart of effective leadership. A leader's ability to foster, nurture, and leverage relationships is not just a skill but a cornerstone of success. Relationships form the very fabric that binds a leader to their team, fostering trust, camaraderie, and a shared vision. Strong relationships built on mutual respect and understanding create an environment where open communication flourishes, enabling a leader to inspire, motivate, and guide their team effectively. These connections extend beyond mere professional interactions; they embody empathy, active listening, and the willingness to connect with individuals on a human level. A leader's capacity to cultivate meaningful relationships not only enhances team cohesion but also fosters an environment of loyalty, collaboration, and innovation. Ultimately, the strength of a leader's relationships often determines the extent of their influence and their ability to steer their team toward collective success.

She also has a lively interest in philanthropy, especially as it has to do with education, witness her multi-year tenure as president and CEO of the College Futures Foundation. Embracing a love for giving back is an indispensable trait in effective leadership. Leaders who possess a genuine passion for making a positive impact beyond their immediate sphere recognize the intrinsic value of serving others. This commitment to giving back transcends mere philanthropy; it embodies a profound sense of social responsibility and empathy. Leaders who prioritize giving back foster a culture of compassion, altruism, and community within their teams and organizations. Their dedication to social causes not only amplifies their impact on society but also inspires their teams to work toward a collective greater good. By leading with a spirit of generosity, these leaders set a powerful example, encouraging others to contribute meaningfully to the well-being of communities. Moreover, the act of giving back often cultivates humility, resilience, and a broader perspective, essential attributes that shape well-rounded and empathetic leaders capable of understanding diverse perspectives and guiding their teams toward a purpose-driven, socially conscious path to success.

RICH LYONS

While Rich Lyons and I were talking on Zoom, I realized his passion for innovation, entrepreneurship and creativity. He talked about the importance of having role models, by saying "you can't be what you can't see. So there's just so many people that don't see themselves in words like venture capital or entrepreneurship or founder or start-up." Many times, I would agree with Rich, because it is hard to become what there is nothing of. Nevertheless, this is a bit more nuanced than what it seems. For instance, what is the difference between a Latino raised in East Palo Alto versus a Latino raised in Latin America? Huge. Abysmal difference. The person raised in Latin America (i.e. Argentina or Brazil) has Latino role models, because the CEOs, engineers, doctors and PhDs in that country are Argentinian or Brazilian. Nevertheless, the Latino raised in East Palo Alto doesn't see CEOs, engineers or doctors who happen to be Latino. Get it? It's a very different world. Moving on, it's also key for pioneers to take the leap of faith and become the first ones. Like my friend Micelle K. Lee who became the first female to lead the US Patent and Trademark Office. When I was 21, I didn't see Hispanic angel investors my age. I didn't see limited partners of venture capital funds who happened to be Latino, first-gen immigrants, so what? I took the leap of faith. Here I am. Became a venture investor at the age of 21 in Silicon Valley.

"What does being an entrepreneur look and feel like?"

Lastly, during my conversation with Rich Lyons, we talked about the importance of having a new solution for inclusion. We could start with language. For example, he mentioned how in the past the "I am a UC Entrepreneur" campaign mostly attracted White males. Makes sense right? They changed the competition to "I am A UC Change-Maker" and guess what?! You have more people of color! More immigrants! More females participating!

"We need something new in the mix to make people feel really included."

During his tenure at the University of California Berkeley, Rich Lyons served as professor of economics and finance, as acting dean and as dean at the Haas School of Business before being named the university's first chief innovation and entrepreneurship officer in 2020.

In our interview as we discussed how Belonging/Inclusion/Diversity/Equality and Innovation/Entrepreneurship can and should co-create, he described at length the new, trademarked Berkeley Changemaker™ initiative, the driver of which is a summer course for incoming freshman as well matriculated students, described in the catalog this way:

For generations, people like you have come to Berkeley to leave their marks on the world, questioning the status quo as they think, and act, beyond themselves. Our Course 12 will activate your passions and help you develop a sharper sense of who you want to be, providing the tools you'll need along the way. Whether you want to start your own company, launch an NGO, discover your passion, or learn how to effect positive, lasting change from wherever you are, our Berkeley Changemaker™ community has a place for you.[5]

In a 2018 article he wrote as a *Forbes Magazine* contributor, Rich directly addressed the subject of distrust and recommended three ways corporate leaders might improve the situation.[6]

1. Whether you manage, mentor, sponsor or coach, focus on longer term goals, even if they might be further into the future, as in "I believe you have the temperament and ability to learn and improve that will one day make you a great CFO of this company...."

2. Move from being a "purpose consumer" to a "purpose creator," which he defines as "someone who appreciates the larger mission of an organization—how it fundamentally affects people's lives—and is able to connect the organization's activities, strategies and storytelling to that purpose."

3. Question the status quo—look for a better way.

Rich clearly believes that belonging/inclusion is not only critical, but necessary, for individuals and the companies for which they work—at whatever level. As he puts it: "You can't be what you can't see."

LORI CASTILLO MARTINEZ

Being relational over transactional and having the passion to learn about others' agendas has taken me a long way. Do I have my own agenda? Yes. I'm a driven entrepreneur. But that doesn't mean I'm not interested in other people's agendas. What I mean by this, is that when I meet someone I try to be a student of them, learn from them, take the good things, learn from their mistakes. When I met Lori, she was VP of Employee Relations—today, she is the Chief Equality Officer at Salesforce. Wow! Congrats Lori. We bonded over the same sport events we attended such as the US open in New York for tennis and how she lived in Germany—I shared how my uncle David moved to Germany at the age of 19 to study electrical engineering and work for Siemens. Moving on, Lori's son Joaquin ended up interning for Pan Peru as a marketing intern. Super grateful for Joaquin for improving our digital presence. As you can see, we can all mutually benefit from relationships. By thinking outside the box and asking for help. You don't need to be a CEO to help another CEO. You don't need to be a C-suite executive to help another C-suite executive. All I did, was to ask Lori, how can I help you? Or your kids? Or your husband?

Calling Lori Castillo Martinez's career path "moving up through the ranks" is a bit like calling a climb to Mt. Everest a "hike." She began with just over eleven years at Intel, first in human resources, with a focus on relocation, then global project management, to be joined by ethics and compliance and internal audit. Then after a year as director of ethics and compliance at VMware, she moved to McKesson for eight years, including senior roles—as in vice president—in Stuttgart and London. Then, after just over four years with Salesforce, she was appointed executive vice president and chief equality officer in January 2020.

In our interview, Lori stressed the importance of not letting "numbers" drive hiring decisions. She explained that from the groups on which her company focuses—Blacks, Latinos, indigenous communities and women—the number of applications Salesforce receives for openings they post is very low. She was quick to insist that hers is not a company that claims there are no qualified candidates.

"They're there; we know they're there. We are just not savvy enough to reach them. This is not really about the pipeline, it has to do with the network."

Since Lori IS savvy enough to both define the problem and own it, the solution is assuredly on the horizon.

BILL MCDERMOTT

Bill, such a character, such a leader with a big heart. We got introduced via Russ Elmer (General Counsel at ServiceNow). I got invited to speak at ServiceNow during Hispanic Heritage Month of 2021. With hundreds of people live on Zoom, the energy and feedback I got after my FuegoSide chat was outstanding. This fireside chat was one of my most memorable. ServiceNow engineers/sales reps were so engaged during my keynote. What I LOVED about this speech, was that both Russ Elmer (Chief Legal Officer) and Nick Tzitzon (Chief Strategy Officer) were present during this Hispanic event. Let's talk about executive sponsors. After my speech, Russ messaged me on LinkedIn: Thank you for your great presentation to ServiceNow, Pedro. This is terrific! I took advantage of this opportunity to ask for a ten minute Zoom meeting to gain more feedback on my oratory. Russ and I bonded over our passion for waking up early to go swimming. At the end of our conversation, I asked Russ if he could connect me with Bill McDermott (CEO of ServiceNow) given that the first business software I used as a teenager working for a gas station was SAP Business One. Bill was CEO of SAP before being CEO of ServiceNow. Russ opened the door and this was how I met Bill. BTW—Bill is a ball of joy. Thank you Russ for the intro!

Bill McDermott, CEO of ServiceNow, believes in positive—people, programs and perspectives. As he wrote in an article published to promote his company's *Let's Workflow It* podcast, in this case regarding their Vaccine Administration Management (VAM) solution: "I've always believed that the world's biggest challenges are also its biggest opportunities." And then: "If you always do what you always did, you'll always get what you always got. That's not good enough; it's time for change."[7]

There are lots of leaders who define themselves as "people persons." McDermott takes another tack altogether: he talks about how he feels about people. For example, in our interview we were discussing various mutual friends: Pat Gelsinger, Teresa Briggs, and Anita Sands (all of which were writing contributors/foreword writer/introduction writer for *Differences That Make a Difference*). McDermott's summary line? "I consider it a privilege to be in the same ecosystem with such incredible people." And from his book, *Winner's Dream: A Journey from Corner Store to Corner Office*: "...if a vision is not supported by the workforce, even the most brilliant ideas risk being nothing more than light bulbs in a basket." And on inclusion: "People don't care how much you know until they know how much you care."

For the first 100 days after assuming his position at ServiceNow, Bill traveled the world. His goal was to get to know in a face-to-face setting as many employees as possible, and to add customers to that mix when he could. As he explains his focus: "The big idea is to be completely consumed by things outside the building(s) where you work. When enough people care about a cause and are all in it together, they can do amazing things."

Finally, he offers what he describes as the TOP IDEA in his book:

> ## "Trust is the ultimate human currency. You gain trust in drops and lose it in buckets."

JOE SIMITIAN

My good friend Joe. We met through the Silicon Valley Leadership Group as early as 2015 when I was a member of the Working Council as the founder of SmileyGo. At the time, Joe was the Supervisor of Santa Clara County, better known as Silicon Valley. Carl Guardino put us in touch by intentionally sitting us next to each other during one of the SVLG CEO events. Joe and I both went to Berkeley, we both have the "get it done" mentality without being perfectionists, we both love Salvadorian food and we share Christian Catholic values too. Also, did I forget to say we also share a Stanford affiliation? Anyway, too many things in common. The first time I met Joe, he was speaking at an SVLG event. Such an eloquent speaker, I was 19 years old, I was like WOW! I would love to SPEAK like that in the near future. I had a dream. Little did I know that in a few years I would be making six figures a year out of public speaking keynote gigs at Fortune 500 companies: Microsoft, JP Morgan Chase, Oracle and Meta are a few of the many companies who pay me to give keynote speeches on my immigrant entrepreneurial story. Around the same time I met Joe Simitian, I also met another Armenian friend Mary Papazian, President of SJSU (San Jose State University). Little did I know that Joe was also Armenian! I always enjoy learning the cultural backgrounds of my friends so I can better connect with them, learn about their heritage, send a message during an important cultural holiday for them or even write them a small thank you card. Those things go a long way! For example, if you know one of your connections is a devout Christian, make sure to send a Happy Easter card! Or if you know one of your mentors is Dominican, make sure to text her on February 27th wishing her a Happy Independence Day. These small details go very very far in life. This is how I built my network from scratch in Silicon Valley! Being a student, being a learner of my human relationships. Being intentional in keeping in touch and bonding with them.

ENDNOTES

[1] https://www.pewresearch.org/fact-tank/2022/03/09/majority-of-workers-who-quit-a-job-in-2021-cite-low-pay-no-opportunities-for-advancement-feeling-disrespected/

[2] https://www.mckinsey.com/business-functions/people-and-organizational-performance/our-insights/what-employees-are-saying-about-the future-of-remote-work#

[3] https://www.nytimes.com/2021/07/20/business/remote-work-pay-bonus.html

[4] https://asianpacificfund.org/what-we-do/awards/chang-lin-tien-education-leadership-award/2020-recipient-tsujae-king-liu/

[5] https://classes.berkeley.edu/content/2021-summer-ls-c12-001-wbl-001

[6] https://www.forbes.com/sites/richlyons/2018/03/15/in-an-era-of-distrust-here-are-three-ways-to-transform-your-organization/?sh=3b5f2897fe12

[7] https://www.linkedin.com/pulse/dreaming-big-convert-vaccines-vaccinations-bill-mcdermott/

CHAPTER SIX

Making Remote Work: Incorporate... Support... Promote Inclusion

—

Technology has taken a role front and center in communications—which we have already established as a key element in inclusion—and we could easily write pages about and spend hours discussing issues of training and comfort surrounding the use of such technology, all of it pertinent and valid, but also none of it universally or evenly applicable from one organization to another. What is universal is the open, direct, conscious exchange of ideas.

It is important to recognize that remote work is here to stay, whether it becomes the main work mode, or part of a hybrid solution. One of the biggest challenges it brings is that we will not be able to rely on one of the major elements of face-to-face communication—body language. A huge percentage of how we listen is based on reading body language and capturing all the clues that it sends. We need to develop a digital body language for our organizations and, like with any language that we learn, train our teams, use it, enhance it and lead by example. In her book *Digital Body Language: How to Build Trust & Connection, No Matter the Distance*, author Erica Dhawan helps us understand the issues of today's social interactions that are devoid of the very important non-verbal visual signs and gives us a roadmap to develop and implement a Digital Body Language that in turn can significantly improve inclusion and belonging.

On the Cisco website, we found an article on building resilience that is jammed with helpful information. Yes, it recounts the dramatic increase in the use of its Webex videoconferencing platform, but it openly adds that the rise in technology use quite naturally brings with it a call for greater attention to skillsets, security, and sensitivity to the full-life experiences of customers and colleagues alike. Noting that "ensuring human connection and being flexible are key to success," the writers quote Chintan Patel, chief technologist at Cisco UK and Ireland:

> "You have to ensure employees are getting a balance between being always connected and getting time to themselves...it's about being more aware, giving people the space and opportunity to do what they need to do."

Rich Gore, Senior IT Manager, adds that online remote management tools give workers a way to maintain a close connection with their managers. "Otherwise, people can feel rudderless and ignored."

Empathetic leadership is crucial, of course, in the face of the challenges of such issues as cybersecurity, monitoring work-at-home hours via technology, securing and monitoring multiple employee-owned and operated devices...the list goes on. As the Cisco experts put it: "Connectivity, flexibility, wellness and safety are the foundations of endurance." And what kind of management produces that? It comes from "fully appreciating the feelings and motivations of the workforce."

In a webinar for Nordic Business Forum, Basecamp CEO Jason Fried, whose company had adopted a hybrid model well before the onset of COVID, points out that it is easy "to fall in love with what we're used to" especially when a change is being force-fed as remote work often was with the pandemic. A strong believer that when employees can "work from anywhere" the company is stronger, Fried offers specific ways to maximize comfort and efficiency. For example, to avoid the stress produced by too many meetings, bad enough face-to-face, but arguably worse staring into a screen, no matter what the software he had advises long-form writing. "Remote," he insists, is not just a place; it's a way of working. Office work is like a platform, as is remote work, and one does not port over to the other effectively. Finally, for those managers concerned with evaluation, he proposes evaluating the work, not the working (or, in actuality, the worker).

In an online article on keeping employees engaged in a remote work environment, *Entrepreneur* stresses the importance of making employees see themselves as "part of the company, not just another cog in the corporate machine." Informing employees of company goals and needs so that they see their own contribution(s) is the crucial step for making them feel purposeful. And as we mentioned before, realistic concern for employee well-being involves making sure they set boundaries. Working too much is as much a potential problem as working too little.

Smart companies make certain
their managers know how to balance
being professional with being human.
These are the bosses who celebrate an
employee's success, empathize with
those going through hard times, and
challenge people, even when it hurts.

~ Travis Bradberry

PERSPECTIVES ON POINT

Insights Gained From Personal Interviews by the Authors

SYLVIA ACEVEDO

Sylvia and I got invited to attend the Annual LCDA Convention in the heart of New York in 2022. That was a unique business conference because I went there with San Francisco attire: business jacket, blazer and dress pants. Everybody else was wearing a tie. My great friend Carlos Amesquita (former CIO of Hershey) had my back! He gave me a beautiful dark blue tie. He told me: keep it! Carlos and I agreed to attend the next ATP Cincinnati Masters tournament in Ohio. Thanks to my Peruvian Brazilian friend! Going back to the LCDA Convention, Sylvia was a wonderful speaker at one of the sessions on the future of AI and the power of embracing grit. After her speech, I did the typical PD game: approached her, smiled, shook her hand, talked about how my Peruvian engineer mom raised me, and asked for a selfie. She gave me her contact information, and we connected on LinkedIn. A few weeks later and here we are sitting down on Zoom for a thirty minute interview on the return on inclusion. For those of you who don't know, Sylvia serves on the board of directors of Qualcomm and used to be the CEO of Girl Scouts of the USA. While Sylvia and I were conversing about the value of resilience, she mentioned:

"Resilience is very important...
Fail forward,
rejection is redirection."

It is impossible to disagree with Sylvia, every time I remember a success story in my life I think of how I first got rejected, on how I first made a mistake, but then I bounced back. A story I share during my keynotes goes like this: During my sophomore year, I had culture shock as a Peruvian who would wake up at 6am every day (regardless of the day, holiday, or weekend) for breakfast and eat lunch at noon. Well guess what, Berkeley had brunch starting at 10:30am on the weekends. So LATE! This killed me! I would starve. My solution, to walk the extra mile every day to grab an early Peruvian breakfast at 7:30am at the Golden Bear Cafe. One morning, I saw an elderly businessman wearing a suit. Most tables were busy except for the one with the wise businessperson. Mom would say, surround yourself with the wisest. My name is Pedro, can I eat with you? Sure, my name is Frank Baxter. Frank, why are you here? This cafe is for kids. I'm a trustee at the Berkeley Foundation, our board meeting got rescheduled, I was hungry. With my analytical immigrant antennas, I saw a US flag pin with a Uruguayan flag on his suit. Why are you wearing a Hispanic flag? I used to be the Ambassador to Uruguay under Bush. That's when we started speaking Spanish! We clicked. Two humans from different generations, socioeconomic statuses, and mother tongues. We bonded over Spanish. Frank was curious why I chose Berkeley. I shared that I had a fintech startup that matched companies with nonprofits. He immediately shared he served as the CEO and Chairman of Jefferies. Small world! The Investment Bank CEO met a fintech founder CEO. He asked how I developed the immigrant hunger to start a company, move countries, learn a new language, and he gave me his business card. Every month, I would email Frank the Espinoza newsletter of my academic endeavors, personal stories, and startup challenges. We fostered a relational friendship. We went on walks around the Berkeley campus. Most importantly, I gave back. BILATERAL MENTORSHIP. I asked: Frank, how can I help you? Can you imagine? A 20 year old immigrant entrepreneur asking this millionaire, Ambassador, CEO, and Trustee how he can help him? Boldness. Frank shared how he was hosting a Civics Seminar and wanted to engage more international students. I had lots of fellow immigrant students from Latin America. I shared my network with Frank by inviting my fellow Hispanic students to attend. He was impressed by my intentionality in reverse mentorship, by my tenacity in following up, delivering, and not quitting. I even helped him with Spanish pronunciation! Tenacity. Yes, after years of friendship with Frank Baxter, can you guess who was the first investor in SmileyGo? Who was the first investor in my first tech AI startup? Yes, Frank Baxter. He BECAME my first angel investor for my startup.

Later in our conversation, Sylvia and I talked about the importance of having confidence:

> "I've never been an 'other'
> and I will never be an 'other'.
> That's how I got, I owned my space,
> I owned my mind. And then I said,
> I belong there."

Wise words from Sylvia. We belong here. It's key to have self-confidence, be the architect of your own career in order to succeed as an immigrant, entrepreneur, leader, etc. It was thanks to the confidence that I embraced to ask Frank Baxter if I could eat next to him, if I could share the table with him, if I could get his business card, confidence enabled me to ask him questions. Mom would always say: pregunta, pregunta y pregunta!

PAT GELSINGER

Pat Gelsinger and I go way back. This story emphasizes the story of embracing resilience, grit and creativity. In early 2018, a friend of mine, John Knox, invited me to attend a TBC (Transform the Bay with Christ) event in San Francisco. When I read the agenda, I noticed Pat Gelsinger was the keynote speaker. I googled him— found out he was one of the few CEOs of a publicly-traded company who was a devout Christian. I saw that he was a published author as well. I wanted to attend his lecture. Pat gave a very inspiring speech. After his speech, there was a line of people waiting to get a picture with him and a signed copy of his book: *The Juggling Act*. I had to make a decision: wait fifteen minutes or grab Brazilian Steakhouse at Espetus in SF. As a good Peruvian, I opted for food. I knew God was going to open doors for Pat and I to meet. I was determined to talk to him after hearing his keynote at a Transforming the Bay with Christ event. The next day, I took a guess at his email. I sent ten emails: nine bounced and one went through. My first email to Pat summarized why I sought his mentorship, "heard your keynote speech, read your book *The Juggling Act*, you're a Fortune 500 CEO, you're open about your faith, you believe in education, we share the same values, I want to learn how to become a better CEO and an author like you via a ten minute meeting." Always ask for ten minute calls to gain advice. As they say, ask for money and you'll get advice. Ask for advice and you'll get money. The next day at 5am I received Pat's reply to my email inviting me to his VMware office in Palo Alto for an early morning meeting. At the time, I lived in the east bay—as a good Millennial/Gen Z I woke up early to drive one hour to get to his office before 8am.

We bonded over our rural backgrounds, respectively in Pennsylvania and Peru. I immigrated to the US believing in the American Dream encompassing failing forward, trying again and again, and taking risks. Can you guess a year later in 2019, who was the foreword writer of my book *Differences That Make a Difference*? Pat Gelsinger.

During our conversation about *The Real ROI*, Pat mentioned the importance of AI:

> ## "Every new technology has destroyed jobs and created jobs....AI will be no different.... The question is, do you know how to use the new tools? So you're part of the job creation as opposed to the job destruction on the other side."

When it comes to the future of skills, I cannot agree more with Pat. We have to be on the right side of the future, we have to learn and embrace the skills that will be valuable for the AI age. Hence, we must be intentional in teaching these skills especially to the underserved communities so they don't get left behind. Later in our conversation, we talked about the importance of failing forward. Pat said

"You learn far more in failure than you do in success...sometimes you just have to fail hard."

This is so true, many times, especially here in Palo Alto people teach you to fail fast. But more than failing fast we must fail hard to truly learn.

I saw in Pat the older version of who I want to be—a global leader, an entrepreneur connected to his heritage. Pat's guidance resonates through my work:

"Never ever be ashamed of your goal, be unabashedly passionate about your objectives. You are giving others the opportunity to join your dream. You are giving people the privilege to support you. Don't be shy Pedro!"

JAMES C. MORGAN

Jim Morgan and I met through my dear friend Dana Ditmore, former executive at Applied Materials. Dana and I became good friends through Jorge Titinger, my co-author. We grabbed a meal together in downtown Palo Alto in 2019, and since then, we hit it off. Thanks to Dana, I got my first board of directors opportunity as a 25 year-old in Silicon Valley: by joining the board of Silicon Valley Tech Academy. Thank you Dana for being a door-opener in my life!

Sometimes when you write a book you are allowed to choose the title; on other occasions the publisher's marketing gurus have the honor. Those of us who have the pleasure of knowing Jim Morgan would argue pretty strongly that the title of his book—part autobiography, part business know-how—is his choice. Sounds just exactly like what he would say: *Applied Wisdom: Bad News Is Good News If You Do Something About It*. By the time he left Applied Materials, after nearly thirty years as CEO, plus a few more as chairman of the board, the company was operating in eighteen countries and employed more than 15,000 people.

And while Applied Materials is solidly in the "tech" arena, Jim's ideas apply to all kinds of organizations, including, he is quick to point out, not-for-profits. In our conversations about what will work best in a US corporate culture highly unlikely to return to its pre-COVID model and probably more dependent than ever on the kind of inclusion that will spark innovation, Jim is direct, as always, with his trademark mixture of analysis and enthusiasm.

He stresses the need to focus on the data behind what kind of inclusion create innovation, and then move on to what he calls "the next level of maturity"—a sense of belonging. He bases his recommendation on his own experience, some data-driven, some anecdotal.

"In my family, we never spoke negatively of anyone. It was respect for all."

Adding that the second version of his book suggests a three-part strategy of culture, planning and implementation, he notes that currently the idea is to promote mindfulness, which in turn produces better thinking from the staff, and typically a 10% increase in innovation.

REBECA OBREGON-JIMENEZ

Corporate Vice President of the Advanced SiP Group at Amkor Technology, Rebeca Obregon Jiminez has a rich mix of educational and professional achievement along with some personal experiences that form her perspectives on inclusion. Noting that her early classroom was in a male-dominated international school where English was the language of social interchange as well class instruction, she remembers understanding nothing. Though it was not long before she managed to learn English, her early struggles gave her a preference for numbers, which, in turn, made her goal-oriented with a strong focus on achievement. It could be argued, too, that numbers specify instead of describing characteristics. As Rebeca recalls:

> "When I arrived in the USA I heard the word 'minority,' and I was told that I belonged to two of the minorities that existed, one for being a woman and the other for being Hispanic (Latina), but in my head I could only think that each person is different, no matter if you are Mexican, American, Hispanic, Latino etc."

Led by the firm conviction that since difference is inherent and culturally defined, the focus must be on a collaborative environment that makes room for all involved to demonstrate their strengths, she is firm in her insistence that her own leadership style and success have devolved from that perspective:

> "The most important thing is to have an attitude of cooperation, being humble and trying to get along with everyone, to earn the respect of people, but collaborating, listening to different points of view to decide.... Let your work speak for itself and show what you are, what personality you have, and let people discover that they want to work with you regardless of your background. This is how I have managed to achieve everything I have set out to do, no matter if I am the only woman, and even more, the only Hispanic woman in a place. What matters is that I am demonstrating my capabilities to achieve the work that is required, I can control what I do, but not what the world thinks of me, so I work to do what I do in the best possible way."

Rebecca is all about actions. She is a doer. We talked about the importance of being coachable and down-to-earth. In our interview she shared about her former bosses and best practices when it comes to embracing a humble attitude:

> "During my professional career, I have had good bosses, but I think that more than anything, it is the attitude of cooperating and being humble, being able to help everyone and earn the respect of other people by collaborating and listening to all points of view, that has gotten me to where I am today, it is my style and it is the style that I have adopted as a manager, and this has led me to have opportunities that I have not sought, but have given me a way to be where I am."

I agree with Rebeca since being down to earth has benefited me in multiple ways. Being open to feedback, having an open door policy has helped me grow as an entrepreneur. I remember the first time I was interviewing for board positions, I asked for feedback the first time I didn't get it. A mentor said: "you didn't speak the board language, you didn't speak the executive lingo and board speech." He was right. I was open to his feedback, applied his feedback and got the board position the next year.

"When I arrived to the United States,
I heard the word minority, a word that
I never understood, because for me
it was normal, I was me or a person,
I was simply a person, not for belonging
to a different group I was part of a
minority, however, for the rest of
the world I was a double minority,
since I was a woman and a Latina."

I 100% related with Rebecca when she shared her story during our interview. For me, it was the same, in Peru I wasn't the minority given that many Peruvians are mestizos (trigeños). In Peru, the CEOs, doctors, engineers, lawyers were Peruvian. Unlike here in the U.S., where for a young Hispanic kid growing up in Silicon Valley or Texas they don't really see many CEOs who happen to be Hispanic, they don't see many doctors who are Latino or tech founders who are Latin. I remember the first day of classes at Stanford, I was the only Peruvian in the room, and one of two Hispanics in the room. Same for Berkeley, during my two years of business school at Haas, I was one of the very few Hispanics in Berkeley. During my two years at Harvard Business School, I was one of the very few Latinos in the HBAP program.

DHEERAJ PANDEY

Dheeraj and I met through the Silicon Valley Leadership Group when I was 20 years old, being the CEO & founder of SmileyGo. At the time, he was the Nutanix CEO and we both served on the CEO Airport Committee at SVLG. Dheeraj and I share the same core family values, we bonded when I shared how often I traveled to Peru to care for my mom. He also shared how he cares for his mom in Los Gatos.

It is all too easy to make the mistake of seeing a "data dude" as letting his (or her—dudess?) focus on complicated programming and the potential of artificial intelligence edge out any concern for people, be they employees or customers, shareholders or vendors. Lest you fall into that trap, meet Dheeraj Pandey, co-founder (in December 2020) and CEO of DevRev, a company he describes as "helping developers build the earth's most customer-centric companies." Already piling up top ratings from employees, DevRev is solidly on the side of attracting talent and using inclusion to build an environment of growth and achievement. Let's not forget Dheeraj Pandey was the CEO of Nutanix for several years and is also part of the board of directors of Adobe. Truly admirable! As the website explains:

> People are at the core of DevRev. We are eager to invest in your potential to create the future of software development together. If you have a deep passion for building and a relentless pursuit for perfection, you are one of us.

Dheeraj does more than "walk the walk"; he climbs the hills. For a leader, he says, "Honesty is not enough. You need to include vulnerability; authenticity." He adds that it is vital to "stay grounded," lest the trappings of success make one into a different person.

As Dheeraj sees it, the US business culture is undergoing a basic culture shift. "Ten or twenty years ago, it was all about shareholders. Now we also think of employees and customers." And how does being value-driven make one a better leader? "For one thing, it informs and improves the process of letting go. "One of the most difficult things to do as CEO is determine the appropriate timing to let go. Essentially, you have to take empathy to the next level."

MICHAEL RAO

Let's talk about the power of relationships. Michael Rao and I met through a wonderful friend of mine, someone I truly admire: Mary Papazian. Mary and I met ten years ago when I was a first-time tech founder in Silicon Valley. Mary was one of the 100 CEOs/Presidents I interviewed for my first book, *Differences That Make a Difference*. At the time, she was the President of San Jose State University. As Mary and I got to know each other, she learned that my sister Karina Espinoza (who also did undergrad at Stanford) went to Virginia Commonwealth University for medical school in Richmond, Virginia. That's when she said, oh you should meet my friend Michael Rao who's the President of VCU! When Michael and I met for the first time, we clicked. We bonded over family values and servant leadership principles. We met during the pandemic via Zoom. Turns out that he was the President of Mission College, a community college next to my house in Sunnyvale. I bought my first house at the age of twenty-six in Silicon Valley, and he was the President who built the campus twenty years ago!

Small world. During our interview, Michael and I talked about the importance of embracing entrepreneurial leadership and how that will help any student (any human) to grow professionally, emotionally and socially. As Michael said it:

"Even if everyone doesn't become an entrepreneur, they need entrepreneurial skills."

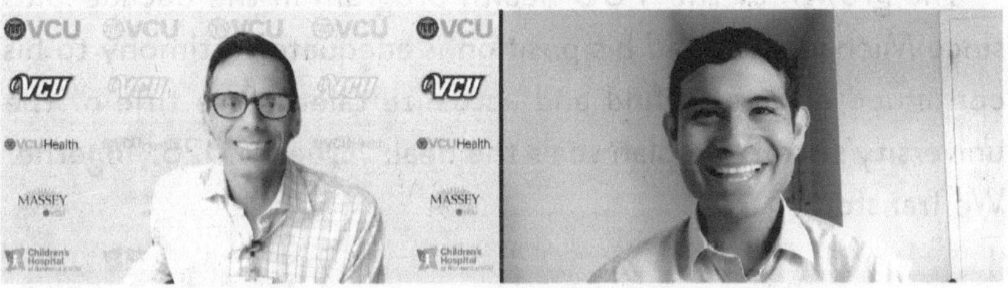

When he became president of Virginia Commonwealth University and VCU Health Center in 2009, Michael Rao had already spent more than fifteen years in senior academic roles: dean of cultural and technical arts, then president at Mission College in the San Francisco Bay Area; chancellor and tenured professor at Montana State; and president and tenured professor at Central Michigan. Do not assume from that, however, that this is a man who exists in ivory towers. Anything but. Within the VCU community, there are multiple initiatives that bespeak energy and innovation. The Brandcenter, part of the VCU Business School, has garnished accolades throughout the marketing and advertising world. Rao also serves on the board of Activation Capital, an incubator, yes, but so much more.

Born in Boston, Michael was quite young when his father, a physician from Mumbai, India, died. He has a lifelong interest in healthcare and the time and effort he has devoted to growing that program at VCU has produced strong, measurable results. Both Rao's mother and his wife are from India, and he is quite candid when he discusses the insensitivity he has witnessed over the years. Indeed, during his first weeks on campus, walking into university-sponsored social events he himself was mistaken for a valet or a waiter. "Not only does that kind of incident need to be eradicated," he says, "but each person needs to stop putting her/himself down for being Latin...or Asian...or Native American..."

The growth of the VCU health program in the decade-plus since Michael assumed his position is adequate testimony to his continued efforts to find and actualize talent. The title of the university's strategic plan seals the deal: "Quest 2025: Together We Transform."

> The finance world is 100% technologic, if not, you are out.
>
> ~ Alejandro Valenzuela | CEO of Banco Azteca

CHAPTER SEVEN

Taking Trust From Imperiled to Imperative

—

No matter the organization or the arena, when established practices, policies and procedures undergo significant change that is neither planned nor anticipated, it is not uncommon for what had been standard working relationships to disintegrate and collaborative networks to fray. When the change is as basic as deciding who works when and where, there are basic questions of accountability. As we mentioned previously, when employers saw the reports of a significant hike in productivity produced by remote working arrangements, they were eager to make the Work From Home (WFH) paradigm more than a pandemic-length phenomenon. But there are glitches, many of them connected with the issue of trust. Consider questions such as:

> What message does using a piece of software to measure the amount of time an hourly employee is online send to that employee?

What about retention? The logistical disruption that changing jobs introduces when the employment is on site disappears with WFH arrangements. And the interpersonal connections that underpin employee loyalty are not nearly so robust. Turnover is expensive indeed. The Gallup organization estimates that replacing an employee can cost from one-half to two times the employee's annual salary.[1]

And then there is the tension between the employee and employer points of view regarding rates of pay particularly in metropolitan areas. Professor Goolsbee summarized the potential effect in his *New York Times* article this way:

According to the Census Bureau[2], Americans spent, on average, a record 55.2 minutes a day commuting in 2019, before the pandemic. One in ten spent more than 2 hours a day traveling to and from work. In dollar terms, not having to commute 5 to 10 hours per week is like getting a 10 to 20% raise. For someone with average hourly earnings in 2021 (over $30[3]), that time is worth $7,000 to $15,000 per year. Looked at another way, the monetary value of the saved commuting time would be one of the biggest tax cuts the middle class had ever received. If your pay is higher than average or your commute is longer, your benefit is worth even more.

But he then asks if employers will take "the bounty" for themselves:

It's not hard to see how employers could. With all the commute time freed up, what is to stop them from simply asking employees to work longer from home—to prepare that report before the meeting starts in the morning or to answer emails or contact clients or file those forms at all hours of the day or night?[4]

In a June 2021 study of management practices that matter in inclusive workplaces, McKinsey highlights seven organizational systems, noting that the move toward remote work makes such systems particularly important. Thank you McKinsey for these seven organizational systems:

1. SELF-EXPRESSION: Creating a space for all employees to express themselves in ways that are personally meaningful.

2. PROTECTIVE MECHANISMS: Discouraging, inappropriate, disrespectful, or biased behaviors at work and providing employees a safe way to report such behaviors.

3. CONNECTION OPPORTUNITIES: Creating opportunities for employees to get to know one another and develop interpersonal relationships across the organization.

4. COLLECTIVE IDENTITY: Uniting all employees around an over-arching purpose.

5. MERITOCRACY: Creating objectives and consistent processes for personnel decisions and merit-based rewards.

6. RESOURCE ACCESSIBILITY: Providing all employees with equal access to information, opportunities, and relationships they need to be successful.

7. WORK-LIFE SUPPORT: Showing appreciation for employees' non-work demands, responsibilities, and interests.[5]

Obviously, WFH diminishes, if it's a hybrid with a selected number of in-office days, or disables, if it's fulltime, the employee "water-cooler collegiality." Therefore, extra efforts are necessary both to keep employees engaged, and to fend off episodes of employer/employee misunderstanding and distrust. Some companies are implementing the following:

- Strengthening the activity levels of and the budget for ERGs.

- Creating out-of-office gatherings, e.g., tickets for sporting events, concerts, TED talks.

- Structuring training and other meetings to be available both face-to-face and remotely.

- Offering training as needed for interfaces such as Zoom, Teams or Webex.

- Bolstering the length, variety, and frequency of different types of written (online or on paper) employee communication vehicles.

Some of these initiatives can be much more effective when the existing level of employee expertise is carefully assessed. A simple, but potent, example is the choice of Zoom "view." Unless the gallery view is engaged, only the person speaking can be seen, which may well have a significant effect on group cohesion. And there is some research that suggests looking at their own image when they are speaking can be stressful for employees, so opting out of the video capability could be recommended.

It could be argued that never has it been more important to assure that every employee, at whatever level, feels seen, heard, and valued. And with the divide between work and family obligations no longer defined by place (or in some instances, time), many consultants suggest employers pay special attention to setting, communicating, and adhering to a clear work schedule. Indeed, research suggests that an employee working remotely may lengthen rather than shorten her/his workday. Please note, though, that "setting a work schedule" is defined as an agreed-upon number of hours worked. Insisting that the work be accomplished during specific hours of the day is counter-indicated, especially when parents are struggling with childcare issues.

Similarly, the communication with customers, investors, vendors, and community leaders, if front-line employees are working remotely, can go awry without careful and consistent attention to timeliness and tone, as well as content.

At the core of all these issues is the question of who trusts whom—how that is recognized or expressed, when it matters most, and how to create an environment that is open and safe for all who enter or work in it. Regarding trust, particularly as it is articulated by leaders, David Horsager serves in multiple roles: advisor, author, consultant, entrepreneur, professor, speaker and strategist. His clients/customers/readers/students represent a full array of organizational settings—academic, corporate, govern-mental, not-for-profit, and individuals who are learning because they wish to strengthen their own skill sets or relationships.

Horsager identifies what he terms the "8 Pillars of Trust":

1. CLARITY: We trust what is clear and have trouble with ambiguity.

2. COMPASSION: When someone clearly cares about others, we see them as worthy of our faith.

3. CHARACTER: Choosing to do what is right instead of what is easy is a hallmark of being trustworthy.

4. COMPETENCY: You've heard it: "She knows what she's doing and how to do it, so it works."

5. COMMITMENT: Rough road? He clears it or finds another. Giving up isn't an option.

6. CONNECTION: Friendship matters.

7. CONTRIBUTION: Promises become results; the way to "We did it"; is wide open. Yes!!!

8. CONSISTENCY: What makes all the others work best.

Author's Note: If you are working through this as a part of a book club or group at work, try breaking the group into eight teams and giving them each one of the words. Try a brainstorming exercise where you have each team describe what the word means to them. Have them share with the group and encourage a larger conversation about these pillars.

Horsager's book, published in 2009, detailing these pillars is titled: *The Trust Edge: How Top Leaders Gain Faster Results, Deeper Relationships, and a Stronger Bottom Line*. A dozen years later he followed up with *Trusted Leader*, articulating the concepts through the perspective of one CEO. Then there is the annual research publication *The Trust Outlook*. There and in the more recent book, we found lots to "chew on." Consider just these three:

1. Ask folks why they want to work for a specific organization, and trusting the leadership comes in first, ahead of a raise, good benefits, a fun work environment, or more autonomy.

2. The number of Americans who have invested $100,000 or more based purely on their trust in someone else tops 12 million.

3. Most millennials say knowing they could trust their leadership would make taking a pay cut acceptable.

Other authors/speakers/consultants agree with the primacy of trust, as well as of openness, or what today we often refer to as transparency. Stephen M. R. Covey, (son of the well-known author of *The Seven Habits of Highly Effective People* and president and CEO of the Covey Leadership Center) has at this writing three popular titles: *The Speed of Trust: The One Thing that Changes Everything*; *Smart Trust*; and *Trust & Inspire: How Truly Great Leaders Unleash the Greatness in Others*. Covey, like many other authors (John Hennessey among them), also stresses humility. As he writes in:

The Speed of Trust: The One Thing that Changes Everything:

A humble person is more concerned about what is right than about being right, about acting on good ideas than having the ideas, about embracing new truth than defending an outdated position, about building the team than exalting self, about recognizing contribution than being recognized for making it.

Very clearly, a trustworthy person.

So, what is it that we can do to drive inclusion in this remote/ hybrid business world that we move in today? We must be intentional about communicating in a way that creates trust with our teams. Being mindful that technology limitations and traditional meeting norms can present obstacles to communication, make sure that you are deliberate in the tone you set at work. We need to be mindful of the message that our actions send as well. Jorge recounts an incident where he was having a conversation with the CEO of a Fortune 100 company as they were walking around Stanford campus. The CEO had a sticky-note pad and would leave a note in every empty cubicle or office she saw that essentially said: "where are you?" and signed it. Jorge asked what the real concern behind these notes was, and the response was that the company had invested heavily in real estate to provide everyone with a nice place to work, yet people did not show up to their workspace. After pointing out to the CEO that she was solving the wrong problem (too many buildings), Jorge asked her what kind of message around "trust" was she sending to the employees who received the note? After reflecting upon that question for a short time, they retraced their steps and removed the sticky-notes. No damage done but imagine if you were one of the employees who got a note, and you had arrived early in the morning to work and were attending an important meeting, then returned to your workspace to find such a note...I am sure you would not have felt trusted by your CEO.

> Transparency,
> honesty,
> kindness,
> good stewardship,
> and even humor,
> work in businesses at all times.
>
> ~ John Gerzema

PERSPECTIVES ON POINT

Insights Gained From Personal Interviews by the Authors

JAMES JONES

General Jones and I met through a close friend of mine: Carlos Gutierrez, former US Secretary of Commerce. Evidently, Carlos has written the foreword of this book. Carlos introduced me to General Jim Jones on a bases of trust. That's the power of relationships! Relationships are trust-based. Our sponsors are our social brokers who open doors for us. Have you heard of the metaphor the third door? There's always a third door to get things done. Unfortunately, many of us have been unaware of the third door. Let's look at my case, I had a 2.6 GPA at Berkeley, dropped out of the Full IB Program in high school, dropped out of a Stanford academic quarter, failed managerial accounting in business school, but here I am! Resilient. Let's fail forward with trust. For those of you who don't know, General Jim Jones is a retired United States Marine Corps four-star general who served as the 21st United States National Security Advisor from 2009 to 2010. During his military career, he served as the 32nd Commandant of the Marine Corps from 1999 to 2003, and Commander, United States European Command and Supreme Allied Commander Europe from 2003 to 2006. Jones retired from the Marine Corps on February 1, 2007, after forty years of service. Fun facts about General Jones is that he served on the board of directors of The Boeing Company, Chevron Corporation, and General Dynamics. We met in his company's Jones Group International LLC headquarters in Tysons Corner, Virginia for an in-person interview. We started sharing about our world travels endeavors. I thought I was a well traveled leader (40 countries) yet General Jones has been to over 100 countries. When I asked him about the power of resilience in leadership he shared:

"We really have two choices in our daily lives: to overcome or to give up. Giving up is not in my DNA."

100% with him, I couldn't agree more. When I was a child in Peru, I would read the newspaper *El Comercio* to find out about the World Economic Forum, the annual meeting in Davos. As a young boy in Peru, I said 'one day' I will be there. That dream started in Lima, was nourished and grew. As I was in business school in Berkeley Haas, my professor Kellie A. McElhaney mentioned WEF Davos for a case study on the fourth industrial revolution. The dream was still there! I found out WEF had a Global Shapers division for young adults. I applied to get into the San Francisco hub. Got rejected. I applied to the Oakland hub. Got rejected. I finally got an interview for the San Francisco hub, apparently, I passed the interview. Yet to find out later, from a phone call that a mistake had been made, there was a quota, even though I had been accepted, there was not enough space. Yet, I continued, I failed forward to find out there was a Palo Alto hub. I applied, and finally got in. A year later, the opportunity to run for Vice Curator opened (I wasn't intending to run, the ideal candidate had a startup problem and couldn't run, she asked me to run). At the age of 27, I was in Davos for the World Economic Forum Annual Meeting. Dream came true. Since then, I've been going to Davos every January. When I shared with General Jones how the U.S. changed my life, he expressed:

"The United States still has the greatest opportunity for individual and collective success on the face of the planet."

It is so true. In the U.S., we have the biggest opportunity for collective success. I was raised in Peru. A few people know I did one semester of 5th grade in Nashville. Growing up in Peru, my hyperactivity was seen as a negative trait. I had a behavioral clipboard, every class the teacher had to monitor my conduct. I asked too many questions. I over-participated. I talked too much. However, in Nashville my teacher Ms. Leigh Parrish congratulated me for it! During the first week of class, my classmates asked: Pedro where are you from? Peru! Where's Peru? South America. Where is South America? South of North America. Huh? That's when I stood up in class: "Hey guys! I'm Pedro, from Peru, South America which is south of North America. We have the Amazon rainforest, the Andes mountains and the pacific coast." This was my first speech. Everyone applauded. My teacher said my boldness, initiative, and willingness to ask questions were positive traits of my character: leadership. That completely changed my self-awareness of my leadership traits! The U.S. changed my life for good, enabled me to dream, to view my distinctive personality qualities as positive traits. That was my first speech. Today, I am grateful to say that Fortune 500s pay me five figures to deliver keynote speeches about my immigrant story. That story inspired General Jones. Last but not least, when I asked Jim Jones about embracing grit, he said:

"The odds are that if you're willing to work hard and have a certain level of talent and curiosity, you can do just about anything you want and be successful."

BRIAN REAVES

Brian Reaves is ahead of the curve—again. When UKG (Ultimate Kronos Group) appointed him "Chief Belonging, Diversity and Equity (BDE) Officer," he became the first we know of to have the word "belonging" in his title. Not that the role is unfamiliar to him, of course. If anything, belonging, inclusion, diversity and equity, especially as they apply in the technology segment of the US economy, is Brian's "schtick." Prior to being at UKG, Reaves served as the Chief Diversity Officer at Dell. He has written widely on the subject, about which he is as passionate as he is perceptive.

When we spoke, he was also exceptionally forthright. Early in our discussion he remarked that during his youth, most of his friends were drug dealers, and perhaps in part because of that during his fourteen years in Silicon Valley he has "always tried to find ways to give those in lower socio-economic levels access."

As he has both analyzed and operated BDE efforts in technology-focused corporations, he has identified what he terms the "frozen middle" of the traditional bell-shaped curve. The extremes, he says, are occupied by those who "see this as a zero-sum game" on the one hand, and avidly "want change." What is imperative is to discover what drives the middle.

Brian goes on to identify two strategic elements that can help accelerate the process:

1. Employee Resource Groups, which he sees as "pillars of community engagement"; and

2. foundational learning.

The latter is specifically designed to discover and address why the vast majority of those in affected groups who are hired never move up from the middle ranks. "What is holding them back?" He recommends "teaching and measuring everything," with special attention to succession and developmental planning.

JOHN ROOS

We met through my great friend Joe Simitian, County Supervisor of Santa Clara in California. Joe connected us over iMessage, for us, the iPhone lovers. I'm beyond grateful for the many leaders in my career who have opened doors, been social brokers and connected me with others! It is truly amazing. Meeting John was AMAZING. I was like, wow, this guy serves on the board of directors of Salesforce, was the CEO of Wilson Sonsini, the most powerful tech law firm on earth, and was the US Ambassador to Japan...really?! Wow! During our call with John, I shared with him how my family business in Peru (Autoespar) works with Toyota: Autoespar is the number two Toyota dealer in Peru, right behind Mitsui. I spoke a few Japanese phrases with John. We both love traveling and learning languages. I personally think learning foreign languages makes you a more open-minded leader, inclusive CEO, and culturally well-versed citizen. I write this as I am learning

Mandarin Chinese every week with a tutor from Wuhan and one of my best Berkeley friends who is from Taiwan. During our phone call, John and I also talked about the difficulty of learning golf. Golf doesn't mold character, it shows character. It shows our true character when we fail, such as when we shank the golf club with the ball. We also bonded given that his son is also called David! David being my middle name. I always try to find ways to relate with people. In the end, these CEOs, ambassadors, and Presidents are human too: they have a mom, dad, sister, brother, wife, son, daughter, husband, etc. John and I shared the struggles of learning Japanese too: it has three alphabets. Wild!

No matter how thorough your research or your preparation, when you agree to take on a position that flies the flag of leadership you may be called upon in ways you simply could not expect. So it was for John V. Roos, when he was sworn in as US Ambassador to Japan in August 2009. Not quite two years later, he was dealing with a 9.0 earthquake, a tsunami, and a nuclear crisis. That hill climbed, he kept on keeping on by leading the creation of the TOMODACHI initiative, a public-private partnership that has since raised more than $50 million dollars and put together 40+ exchange programs, one of the more recent ones hosting nine Japanese female university students enrolled in the TOMODACHI-STEM Women's Leadership and Research Program at Lehigh University in Pennsylvania.

On the corporate side of the ledger, John is a co-founding partner of Geodesic Capital, a late-stage venture capital fund, and CEO of the Roos Group LLC, an investment advisory firm. When inclusion is the subject, however, it is his experience on the board of directors at Salesforce.com. to which he turns. "At Salesforce, trust is a core value," he explains, "as is our theme of 'Success from Anywhere.'"

John reinforces those points by stressing that transparency is critical.

"Every company,
has issues it must face.
If you 'spin it,'
you aren't going to address it."

Then he concludes, "Leaders must see employees as assets. Bringing in diverse candidates for open positions is important, but not enough. Providing mentors, for example, is very effective. Doing this well is an ongoing challenge."

"Trust is really a core value.
And we talk about it all the time,
the fact that trust is core
to everything we do."

Couldn't agree more with John. Relationships are based on trust. If we don't trust our stakeholders, vendors, employees, investors, then why are we in business? I remember when I bought my first home in Sunnyvale at the age of 26. Jack Fuchs (my favorite Stanford faculty member) gave me a 3-day loan to make my down-payment possible. I sold my Meta, AMZN and NVDA stock to buy my first real estate in Silicon Valley. Let's go! Trust! Did we sign a contract? No. It was based on trust.

"You need mentors...
if you have someone above you that
is looking after you, teaching you,
helping you, I have found that to be
very effective in every organization
that I have been in."

Mentors and sponsors are crucial for one's success. As I evaluate my own career, I've seen wonderful mentors such as Guillermo Diaz (CIO of Cisco) and Yamila Harris (Munich Re Insurance executive) who opened so many doors in my career.

"Diversity and inclusion
is incredibly hard,
but incredibly important...
more diverse organizations in every
different way are stronger, more
successful organizations than not."

100% agree with Roos. We need to be intentional when it comes to inclusion. It is really hard, but success doesn't come easy.

SUKHINDER SINGH CASSIDY

If the process of writing a book takes more than a couple of months, and first-person interviews are a primary source of information, the career trajectories of "go-get-em" interviewees can make for multiple rewrites. Knowing, as we do, the—what's that long word?—"indefatigable" Sukhinder Singh Cassidy, we decided on two accommodations: (1) write this perspective as close to the print date as possible; and (2) recognize that even then what we write might be well behind her career curve when you read it. At this writing, much of the media reportage centers around her compelling new book, *Choose Possibility*. Since adequately describing the career path that led to this point could take pages, let's just read how *she* describes it in the book's introduction:

> Today, I'm a technology executive, entrepreneur, and investor in Silicon Valley, the global center of entrepreneurship and wealth creation. Over the past twenty-three years, I've started three companies, served as CEO of two others, and helped grow two of the world's largest tech giants (Google and Amazon). I've participated as an employee, leader, investor, or board member at another dozen plus companies ranging from global brands such as TripAdvisor, Ericsson, Urban Outfitters, and J.Crew to successful digital services such as Stitch Fix, Upstart, and Sun Basket to little-known startups that ran out of money and fell back into the sea. I've been lucky enough to see a company I created (Yodlee) go public and to lead another company (StubHub) to a multibillion-dollar sale. I've been heartbroken to watch a company I poured everything into (Joyus) fail, and naïve enough to join two organizations where I just didn't (OpenTV and Polyvore).

Kinda makes you feel like you ratcheted the speed and slope buttons on your treadmill a couple of bumps too far, doesn't it?

Sukhinder goes on to discuss what makes the idea of risk-taking so daunting to people, beginning with a fallacy she has named "The Myth of the Single Choice," a decision to sign onto an action that is essentially "the *right* choice on a straight shot to glory."

Of the multiple insights Sukhinder aired in our interview, three are particularly relevant and also representative of her extraordinary vision:

1. In developing job descriptions to be used for recruitment it is important to give attention to both skills and prior experience. An effort to create a pipeline that will stimulate inclusion rests on reaching beyond traditional career paths.

2. Ask decision-makers to change how they recruit and hire by going beyond the standard resume for information.

3. When the recruiting process has been adjusted to become more inclusive, its success is dependent on whether the rest of the corporate culture has also widened its lenses.

ALFREDO THORNE

I wanted to say a personal thank you to Alejandro Valenzuela for making the introduction to Alfredo Thorne.

To say that Alfredo Thorne is an economist is a bit like saying Roger Federer plays tennis. Founder of Thorne and Associates, an economic and financial consultancy operating in his native Peru, he also served as minister of economy and finance for his native land.

On the global front, he has direct experience with and has written widely on economic issues throughout Latin America, as well as in Russia, Kazakhstan and Central Europe. At JPMorgan Chase Bank he was a managing director in the Global Research

Department, and from 1987 to 1995, he worked at the World Bank as senior country economist for Mexico and also as senior financial economist with the responsibility for advising former socialist countries as they transitioned from centrally planned to market economies. More recently, he joined the advisory committee of the San Diego-based Institute for the Americas, a group that focuses not only on economic development, but also the integration of the people of the Americas. On the education front, he holds advanced degrees from both Oxford and Cambridge Universities.

All of this is admirable and true, but it could lead you to believe that Thorne is stern and ponderous. Anything but. In fact, he could head the list of people who give the lie to the old saying that an economist is someone who hasn't enough personality to become an accountant. Lively mind, creative thinker, he has direct experience with the global economic community.

He is a pioneer in the landscape of corporate finance and economics with an acute focus on political and international arenas. As the founder of Thorne & Associates, he has carved a niche in elevating businesses by providing unparalleled advisory services and a knack for remaining balanced and neutral. His firm is instrumental in the seamless execution of capital and debt acquisition, particularly for foreign entities and innovative fintechs. Thorne's expertise is not confined to the boundaries of Peru; his influence and services resonate throughout the global economic fabric.

BRIAN TIPPENS

Brian is the honorary Peruvian—his Spanish is flawless and he is full of joy, humility and charisma. Such an eloquent speaker, I am impressed by his knowledge of Peruvian geography. Jorge Titinger and I sat down with Brian to gain his insights on the return on inclusion. Brian and I share our fond memories of attending the World Economic Forum in Davos.

Prior to his appointment in 2021 as chief sustainability officer for Hewlett Packard Enterprises, Brian Tippens had served the company for five years as chief diversity officer. Not surprisingly, he approaches the issue of inclusion with a wealth of learning, much of it what the military might term "boots on the ground." Having now stepped down from that position, he also has the valuable opportunity to evaluate the interplay between the emphasis on transparency in the corporate arena and application in the community, based on his work with groups like Operation HOPE, The Latino Coalition and California Disabled Veterans Business Alliance.

Brian's perspective as an attorney comes to the fore as well, as he candidly addresses what works and what doesn't. "There actually is a danger in moving too far, too fast as we work to assure every voice matters," he told us, "because we can unknowingly be doing so at the expense of some marginalized groups."

As a panel member of the World Economic Forum session on "Bridging the Joy Gap" in January 2020, Brian reiterated the need to follow definition with action, noting that creating a poster on a company's dedication to the health and welfare of employees is only the first step; integrating that intention into the corporate culture is the requisite move.

Getting back to your question,
for us the integration should be
much easier since our roots are
much stronger and more common.

~ Alejandro Valenzuela | CEO of Banco Azteca

ENDNOTES

[1] https://www.gallup.com/workplace/247391/fixable-problem-costs-businesses-trillion.aspx#:~:text=The%20cost%20of%20replacing%20an,to%20%242.6%20million%20per%20year

[2] https://www.census.gov/newsroom/press-releases/2021/one-way-travel-time-to-work-rises.html

[3] https://ycharts.com/indicators/us_average_hourly_earnings

[4] https://www.nytimes.com/2021/07/20/business/remote-work-pay-bonus.html

[5] https://www.mckinsey.com/business-functions/people-and-organizational-performance/our-insights/the-organization-blog/inclusive-workplaces-focus-on-management-practices-that-matter-not-fluff

CHAPTER EIGHT

So Near and Yet So Far

—

In many ways, the hierarchical structure that typifies the corporate environment in our Western culture is framed as a barrier to inclusion, and yet we remain blissfully unaware of the situation. Consider the "perks" that often come with a corner office—a private restroom, in-the-office food service, a special row in the parking garage, business or first-class air travel. C-suite executives are known to speak disparagingly of the "ivory towers" of higher education, yet they are just as isolated on a daily basis, perhaps even more so. To enjoy the advantages and experience the increase to the bottom line that inclusion affords requires real intentionality on the part of leaders. Why? Because unless there is an exchange of information, the introduction of fresh viewpoints and obvious (visible, hearable, consistent) respect for not only each person but also each position, little if anything changes.

Our own Western culture is set up as a hurdle to inclusion. Many times people think, if we had a female CEO or person of color CEO, things would change. But it isn't that easy. For instance, I've worked with a Fortune 500 company in the Midwest, where they have a female COO, where the entire leadership team understands the business case, the ROI for inclusion. Nevertheless, they forgot about mid-management. That's where the rubber meets the road. You can have the most intentional and diverse CEO in the top, with an amazing CFO/COO, but, if your middle-managers aren't trained when it comes cultural intelligence, when it comes to inclusion, the women and people of color won't get promoted. Simple enough, we will get the same results. One person can't change the whole company. It takes a team. That's the opportunity I saw while consulting/speaking at this company, and they followed my advice on providing professional development sessions when it comes to being well versed in cultural intelligence. As a result, after six months, over 75% of their mid-managers were culturally smart, and we saw the numbers rise, when it came to female leadership and people of color leadership. They were getting mentored, but most importantly sponsored. By sponsored I mean, people were vouching for them, wearing their jersey when they were not present: boardroom, hiring room and promoting room.

In their book, *Radical Inclusion: What the Post-9/11 World Should Have Taught Us About Leadership*, Martin Dempsey and Ori Brofman outline six principles for the leader who wishes to create and capitalize on inclusion. To summarize the principles here would not do justice to the strength of the authors' argument. The book is full of comprehensive ideas and calls to action. This is how they describe their 'bottom line':

Inclusion is harder and can be slower, but it is a necessary pre-condition for achieving effective, efficient, and enduring solutions to complex problems.

Yes, inclusion can positively affect fairness and equality in the workplace, which yields greater trust between leader and follower. But more importantly, it's about persistent learning, shared ownership of decisions...It's about developing trust by listening, simplifying, and including.

Trust doesn't mean that you trust
that someone won't screw up—
it means you trust them
when they do screw up.

~ Ed Catmull

PERSPECTIVES ON POINT

Insights Gained From Personal Interviews by the Authors

OMAR ISHRAK

Dr. Omar Ishrak and I met through Sylvana Q. Sinha, I know I've mentioned her several times in the book—and yes—she truly is a wonderful human being, who knows everybody, and is willing to open doors for me. For those of you who don't know, Dr. Omar Ishrak served as the Chairman of Intel Corporation in addition to being the CEO and Chairman of Medtronic—one of the largest medical devices companies in the world. Super impressive back-ground, Omar was born and raised in Bangladesh—the 7th most populous country on earth with nearly 160 million humans. Did I forget to mention he got a PhD in electrical engineering from the University of London? Insane! There is more—prior to joining Medtronic, Omar was the CEO and President of GE Healthcare Systems. When both of us met, my mother Julia had recently had surgery with a Medtronic generator on her chest (DBS surgery for Parkinson's). I shared about my mom's health with Omar, we bonded over caring for loved ones, he shared about his family too. Family first. Small world! He used to be the CEO of Medtronic and my mom had recently gotten a Medtronic battery on her chest for her Parkinsons. We bonded, we built a bridge. Later in our conversation, we talked about the power of decision-making, reminding me of my Stanford days when I took Introduction to Decision-Making, Omar shared:

> ## "I do think that having a clear goal in the end helps you make decisions."

When our conversation evolved to inclusion and belonging, Omar was very wise by sharing:

> ## "Inclusion has to mean that you're bringing two people together... it's not about numbers and metrics only, it's about understanding and valuing different perspectives."

Valuing different perspectives and understanding them! Wow. So true. Many times, companies over-focus on numbers. They just want to see those KPIs, those OKRs, but let's get back to the fundamentals. Are people being understood? How's the value of understanding others? It makes no sense to have these Hispanic/ Women ERGs if these humans are being forgotten, have no budget, no one even understands their problems. Pursuing this further, I have to give kudos to the many companies out there such as Salesforce, Meta, Google, and American Airlines that have Inter-Faith Employee Resource Groups. That is inclusion 2.0. Let's be real, many of our employees come from spiritual backgrounds. Especially our immigrant employees. The U.S. is a country of immigrants. Many immigrants from Latin American, African and Asian countries come with a faith backgrounds. Congrats to Salesforce for creating Faithforce, bringing Christians, Jews, Muslims and others unite to do community service together in the Tenderloin district. This is true inclusion! I've had the honor of speaking at spiritual employee groups at Fortune 500 companies such as Chrsitians@Meta in Menlo Park. It's fascinating to see what companies are doing to make sure to care for their faith-based employees. Further, in our interview, Omar and I discussed the value of grit, he shared:

> ## "Grit starts with a pure belief that you want to do something, have a desire to do it. If you believe in something and want to do it, you'll face ups and downs in many different ways."

Trials are part of life. We have to rejoice through these trials. We have to consider it pure JOY when we face trials of many kinds.

When you have a dream, a belief of what you want to achieve, you will FAIL. Rejections are redirections. Let me repeat it, rejections = redirections. These are blessings in disguise. I remember in 2017, I got the first M&A offer for SmileyGo, it was a larger tech venture who wanted to acquire us for a certain dollar amount. I was 22 years old, full of **P**assion, **D**rive and **E**nergy (my initials) ready to grow the company's revenues, goals, and achievements. In the end, we missed that acquisition opportunity, we couldn't close the deal. At first, I was frustrated, sad and upset. Nevertheless, little did I know that destiny, that the future would bring bigger and better things. My technical colleague Daniel Yee and I ended up joining Abide (Carpenters Code), one of the largest wellness apps in the world based in Menlo Park. In a similar way, the first time I applied to become a US Citizen at the age of twenty-one, I got rejected. Was I frustrated and sad? Yes. Did I stay there? No! It's ok not to be ok. It's not ok to stay there. I moved on. Two years later? I'm a citizen of the best country in the world, a country that opened its doors to my family, to me, to pursue a STEM degree, to create AI startups, write business books, give TED talks, join company boards, nonprofit boards and attend classes at the best institutions in the world: Berkeley, Stanford and Harvard.

SOL TRUJILLO

I have to give credit to Yovany Jerez for introducing me to Sol. Yovany, my good Cuban friend apparently knows everybody—especially the Hispanics must-knows

For many years corporate search committees seeking a new CEO would first clarify whether at the current juncture in the company's growth the skill set of a change agent would be optimal as opposed to that of a leader who minimizes disruption and drama and chooses a culture that is based more on sustaining than radical growth. Now some add a third category: change champion, which is usually defined as someone who supports change heartily but may not have primary responsibility for its execution. Taking the curves with acumen and aplomb as CEO for several businesses (US West (AT&T), Orange S.A., and Telstra, Australia's largest telecom) Sol Trujillo has harnessed change repeatedly building a career that is an amalgam of all those skill sets and at the same time an undeniable model of his basic beliefs.

Perhaps as much as anyone we interviewed for this book, Sol is invested in:

1. clarifying the statistics about and performance of the Latino/a business community in the US;

2. insisting that the potential contribution of Latins has been limited by leaders who erroneously see Latinos as he described it in a Forbes interview as "hard workers, but not sophisticated or cerebral."[1]

During our interview, Sol was very direct when it came to his background and how he called America home: "my family has been here in the United States for almost 500 years. So other than the Native Americans." Trujillo gave me a history lecture: "when the Spaniards came, they landed in San Juan, quickly found there was no gold there...then went to St. Augustine...no gold there...so then they tracked inland. By the late 15th, 16th, 17th they land in Santa Fe, New Mexico, they were colonizing them, brought the priest, they settled. They were settling there 100 years BEFORE the Mayflower landed in the northeast. Most people don't know that part of our history. So my family is from the New Mexico area. When I talk to my American friends, I say 'Welcome to my country,' because what existed in North America was that the Native Americans were nomadic, they didn't create cultures and institutions. In South America and Central America they did, the Incas and Mayans were great civilizations. But up here in North America, the real first colonizers and settlers, builders, were the Spaniards, not the British. Some people say well New Mexico wasn't a state then. Neither was New Amsterdam which is now New York. Neither was Boston. So people don't understand a lot of our history in terms of the reality of it. I always like to talk about this, because I am a very proud American. I like to remind people, that this country when Washington, Jefferson and Adams, were writing the constitution, they formed the government, the name of the country that we now have was named the United States of New Amsterdam, NO, of New London, no, United States of que? America. Does that sound British? Does that sound North English? It's a Latino Name. This country's roots as a named country began with the Latinos, the Spaniards." I was impressed by his facts, numbers and statistics.

LAUREN VACARELLO

Lauren and I met through Krystal Le, a great Stanford friend of mine—I met Krystal through my sister Karina Espinoza (Stanford Class of 2012). Both Krystal and Lauren worked at Box at the time. It's crazy how time flies. We got connected via email and LinkedIn, here we are doing our inclusion interview.

To most of us, M&M stands for a colorful chocolate treat, but when the subject of the conversation is Lauren Vaccarello it more likely represents two of her greatest skill sets: marketing and mentorship.

Well-known in the worlds of entrepreneurship and brand-building, she wears all kinds of hats: angel investor, limited partner (Stage 2 Capital), advisor, public board director, chief marketing officer, author, speaker, and on and on. It's not a surprise that she's able to sum up her core beliefs in one sentence on her LinkedIn site: "Although performance is at the core of who she is as a marketer, she believes businesses need to tell compelling stories and build a brand if they want to own a category."

Early on in our interview, it became apparent that Lauren's skills are joined—and no doubt strengthened—by an intense sense of commitment. And the power of those two together have convinced her that serving on boards of directors, be they corporate or not-for-profit, is a first-rate way to make a difference.

On the corporate front, it is her firm opinion that to be an effective CEO, "you have to give up a lot." Being a board member, she believes, affords greater opportunity to make an impact.

So far as the not-for-profit world is concerned, she is straight to the point. "Working for one of those organizations would drive me nuts, but I can help from a board seat." And help, she does, particularly emphasizing the need to close the gaps around such issues as women's healthcare and poverty.

In May of 2021, when Lauren was serving as chief marketing officer for Talend, she was chosen to be part of the first day of ChargeBee's "Champions of Change" event. The quote the organizers chose to put with her photo on the X (formerly Twitter) feed: "It's important to spend time on making human connections. It's okay to stop a meeting for a few minutes to hear your children come and talk about dinosaurs."[2] Clearly, this is not a unidimensional leader.

And, by the way, since she's a believer in company stories, she probably already knows that those two Ms on the candy DO stand for something: one for Mars, the maker of the candy, and the other for Murrie. In 1941, thinking that the war might well cause a chocolate shortage, Forrest Mars struck a deal with Bruce Murrie, son of William Murrie, then the president of Hershey, for chocolate should he need it. There is branding and then there is branding.

JENNIFER WIDOM

Jennifer and I met through Tsu-Jae King Liu, the dean of Berkeley Engineering. When I was done interviewing Tsu-Jae, I asked the question I always ask: is there anyone in your network you suggest I should meet? This question has taken me far in my career. Tsu-Jae thought of her friend Jennifer Widom. Thank you Tsu-Jae for the kind introduction. We clicked with Jennifer, since the first conversation we had: she told me she had already delivered a speech in Lima, had an alpaca hat and enjoyed Peruvian cuisine. I also ran into her while hiking the Dish at Stanford. Small world!

To begin to do justice to Jennifer Widom's achievements, titles, honors, and awards would require a good bit of space, and we think sends the wrong message—that she is somehow limited to academic pursuits and ideas. Let's just be content with the fact that since 2017 she has served as dean of the Stanford University School of Engineering, she is a professor of both computer science and electrical engineering at Stanford, and—guess what?— her bachelor's degree is from the Indiana University Jacobs School of Music. You know we love it when people do creative pursuits in addition to studying hard skills. While I was studying management science and engineering at Stanford in 2015, I would devote several hours a week playing the grand piano in Lagunita Hall. It's really important to have a creative outlet in order to decompress your stress and pursue fine arts as a way for seeking mental health. Work-life balance is crucial, and I truly admire Jennifer's diverse gifts, not only as an engineer but also as a gifted musician. Meeting with Jennifer reminded me of the quarter when I took computer science 106a at Stanford, learning Python but also participating in concerts, attending acapella concerts, and enjoying the fine arts. Words are not enough to describe how important music has been in my career, as I composed a few songs and launched them in Apple iTunes (Apple Music) when I was a teenager. Today, I close business deals at the country club playing the piano for the Amazon VP of Public Policy in Los Altos. Music opens doors. And yes, engineering as well. Let's focus on our strengths and take creative educational paths that work best for them.

Not surprisingly, Jennifer's acumen and experience have together formed her take on how best higher education can help build the pipeline for successful career pathways for students whose economic, educational or cultural backgrounds present special challenges. She makes two very specific points:

1. Often these students have little if any understanding of how academia works. They are definitely out of their comfort zones when we try to accelerate their learning in a certain direction, introducing an element of risk. What is important is that we recognize that discomfort, and let them settle in comfortably, but *stay in touch*. This can be especially crucial if they have family obligations that put a premium on security and control, in time, money or both.

2. The conventional method of 'defining inclusion' often involves a quantitative approach—measuring diversity solely by the numbers present in a particular pipeline or setting. However, this method fails to capture the depth and essence of what true inclusion and diversity entail, especially in environments such as classrooms and beyond.

    Inclusion transcends mere headcounts; it embodies the essence of varied perspectives, experiences, and backgrounds converging in a cohesive, respectful, and equitable environment. While numbers provide a basic metric, they do not encapsulate the immense benefits that diversity brings to a classroom or any other setting.

    The true value of diversity lies in the wealth of viewpoints and insights it offers. In a classroom, for instance, a diverse student body brings a tapestry of ideas, cultural nuances, and differing approaches to problem-solving. This dynamic mix enriches discussions, challenges preconceived notions, and fosters a more comprehensive understanding of subject matter. It prepares students for a globally interconnected world, equipping them with the skills to navigate diverse perspectives and collaborate effectively across boundaries.

JESSIE WOOLLEY-WILSON

Reed Hastings mentioned Jessie Woolley-Wilson during our interview for *Differences That Make a Difference*. Thank you Reed for mentioning Jessie! Reed was one of the 100 CEOs I interviewed for my first book. Hence, for this second book on inclusion, I had to find a way to talk to Jessie. Let's go!

Have you ever scheduled a meeting with someone you don't know and checked with LinkedIn and that person's employer's website to get some idea of who they are. Quite often you come away knowing about lots of titles, functions, awards, achievements, but very little about what their "This I Believe" statement is.

Not true with Jessie Woolley-Wilson, president and CEO of Dreambox. Check this out from the Dreambox site: "Jessie Woolley-Wilson is driven by a singular belief that all children deserve high-quality learning opportunities, regardless of who they are or where they live."

And then there is this from NPR's *How I Built Resilience* series:

Two Phases: Survive and Thrive. Guided by company values and 3 principles:

1. What do we do to take care of our employees? We want them to be safe and secure.

2. How to take care of our customers—our kids, teachers, school administrators?

3. Take care of our talent (employees) and our customers leads to protecting our company.

When you grow really fast you get stretchmarks. We got stretchmarks.

Tell people what you don't know.

When we broach the subject of how to give employees—especially those who somehow fail to feel completely connected—a sense of belonging despite the distancing that can be part of remote work, it is abundantly clear that this is a woman whose emphasis on the topic is longstanding and heartfelt. She leads with: "We're still just all trying to figure out this diversity and inclusion thing together, and, yes, we've been cashing in on the strong culture we had already built."

One of her primary concerns is that decision-makers might underestimate what she calls the "primal need for communication in person." Technological environments, she points out, "don't provide a way to learn what you learn standing in line at the food truck." There is already a strong articulation of how important Dreambox thinks open, regular communication is. The interior design of a recently purchased office building is centered around creating a workspace that accelerates collaborative exchange.

Jessie puts it simply:

> ## *"Proximity* promotes *understanding,* which in turn leads to *empathy."*

DANIEL GAMBA

> # "We are the largest investor in the world, we manage 10 trillion dollars at BlackRock. In this industry, the percentage of women in asset management represents less than 15%. The percentage of people who invest in bonds and stocks is less than 10%.

Among Latinos and blacks, it is less than 5%."

Daniel and I met in person in the heart of Wall Street in New York. His passion for representation was notorious. He is committed to inclusion. Yet he was realistic about Wall Street's lack of representation when it comes to Hispanics. After we met, we took a photo together and posted it on LinkedIn. Little did I know that our picture was going to get 50,000 impressions on LinkedIn in less than a week. The tricky aspect of Wall Street is that all of these firms are fighting over the same diverse talent. My advice was to search in different places. Not just the Ivy League female/Latina graduates, but also look at Hispanic Serving Institutions and HBCUs. Yes, representation has been increasing in Wall Street but there is a LONG way to go. If our investors don't look like the country's population then, there is a problem. The U.S. is already 20% Hispanic. US-born Hispanics are the 5th largest GDP in the world. That's bigger than India's economy. That's BIGGER than the UK's GDP. US-born Latinos represent an economy the size of nearly Germany's GDP. Wow! Kudos to Daniel for serving as BlackRock's CEO of LATAM. Proud of Peru! Peru represents!

> In the US if I follow the rules,
> if I have the capabilities and
> know how to start a business...
> Then the sky is the limit,
> that's why we talk about
> the American dream.

~ Alejandro Valenzuela | CEO of Banco Azteca

ENDNOTES

[1] https://www.forbes.com/sites/soonyu/2020/09/10/smashing-the-cristal-techo-glass-ceiling-for-millions-of-latinos/?sh=67c8f2553349

[2] https://twitter.com/chargebee/status/1395079973161955331/photo/2

BOOKSHELF

Recently, multiple studies by neuroscientists have confirmed the hypotheses that reading online and reading the printed page differ in terms of comprehension as well as retention. Essentially, most argue that reading print is superior in both cases, though there are also studies that indicate the obverse is true. One theory, though, is almost impossible to challenge, to wit: reading a book to do research often offers readers information in addition to what they seek. If what you're looking for appears on the left page, you're likely to see something more on the opposing page or even as you're thumbing through.

In doing the research for this book, we conscientiously reached beyond the business press to other fields of interest. That was planned and purposeful. But every now and again, a topic, footnote, or URL nearby caught our attention. The library of life beckoned, and we rushed in. As our closing section, then, we offer you a smorgasbord of ideas and genres, not always or even mostly limited to the subject of inclusion. Serendipitous learning often changes the lens through which we approach a decision just as inclusion of different perspectives does.

INSIGHT...FORESIGHT... OVERSIGHT...HINDSIGHT

Seeing is believing, so the saying goes. In his book, *Seeing What Others Don't: the Remarkable Ways We Gain Insights*, published in 2013, cognitive psychologist Gary Klein argues that to help organizations gain more insights it is necessary to dial back what he calls the "War on Error." He explains: "People working in organizations face pressure for predictability and perfection (reducing errors and deviations), which motivates managers...to view insights as disruptive."

What to do? Klein suggests creating a team of "insight advocates" whose job would be to promote practices that encourage discoveries, and who would be encouraged to use stories to share what they learn. He devotes several pages to telling stories of his own that demonstrate the link between stories and insights.

He added other suggestions, of course, including an "Oversight Group, convened as necessary to provide a path around any attempts to block an unpopular view."

Here we have a new version of "inclusion," this time of those who have the courage to promote perspectives and solutions that are not the norm.

Just as there are multiple kinds of sight, there are different kinds of blindness. In his 2014 book, *The Power of Noticing: What the Best Leaders See*, Harvard Business School professor Max Bazerman uses case studies (we like to think of them as stories based on real-world examples) to guide us as readers to see how cognitive blind spots lead to vital information being overlooked or ignored, sometimes with disastrous results (as in the Challenger explosion).

While many books on leadership stress the importance of focus, Bazerman suggests that noticing is at least as important, and maybe even more crucial. The key, he argues, is to not only break bad habits, but develop good ones such as realizing you may be paying attention to the wrong details or letting self-interest get in the way of your recognition of a clear and present danger.

It is easy to overlook what might be called the "Who's Where" effect. In other words, in precisely what corporate culture does one feel or wish to feel included? In his book, *Gut Feelings*, Gerd Gigerenzer, a director at the Max Planck Institute for Human Development in Berlin whose research on cognition was an important source for Malcolm Gladwell's popular book, *Blink*, recalls his own efforts to create a research group "whose members actually talked, worked, and published together—a rare thing." He developed a set of five rules, which he describes as "not verbalized, but acted upon":

1. Everyone on the same plane. He notes that employees on the different floors interact 50% less than those on the same floor.

2. Start on the same footing. Members of his team all started to work the same day.

3. Daily social gatherings.

4. Shared success. When a team member succeeds, they buy the cake, the lunch, etc. for the rest of the group instead of vice versa.

5. Open doors—most importantly the director's.

This book is small;
its potential impact is not.

As we mentioned in our discussion of the importance of trust and as we learned from our interview, John Hennessy has a lot to say about leadership. The titles of the first three chapters in his book *Leading Matters: Lessons from My Journey* tell the tale: 1-Humility: The Basis for Effective Leadership; 2-Authenticity and Trust: The Essential Ingredients for Effective Leadership; and 3-Leadership as Service: Understanding Who Works for Whom. And so far as telling tales is concerned, the title of Chapter 9 is: Storytelling: Communicating a Vision.

In dealing with inclusion, it is easy—and quite common—to overlook the importance of assuring that a person *wants* to be included. Discussing the idea of eliciting such buy-in for a "dream" project, Hennessey insists:

> "When you turn that dream into a vivid story, you make it so attractive and so real that people will want to share it with you by joining your team....
> No one ever enlisted anyone into that kind of effort with a pie chart and some PowerPoint slides. Rather, you need to...share your vision, irresistibly."

As we reported earlier on the book, among the books that address the issue of inclusion directly *Radical Inclusion: What the*

Post-9/11 World Should Have Taught Us About Leadership, by Martin Dempsey and Ori Brofman has a lot to say, much of it delivered in well-crafted stories. And the authors preach what they practice early on in a chapter entitled "The Power of Narrative." Once again, the stories are too rich to abbreviate here, but here's how that chapter ends: "We'll soon see that for companies wanting to effectively engage in a battle of narratives, inclusion is becoming the new way of being heard."

COUNTING IT OUT

If you are buying a new car, even if you've been driving for decades and this new one is basically an updated version of the one you're trading in, you are not likely to throw away the manual the salesman made sure is in the glove compartment. In much the same way, whether you're a seasoned veteran or a newbie in the World of Inclusion, a well-written, comprehensive guidebook is important. *The Inclusion Dividend: Why Investing in Diversity & Inclusion Pays Off* by Mark Kaplan and Mason Donovan is just such a book. Again, some entertaining stories to give life to established principles, tactics and strategies.

Another such book is *The ROI of Human Capital: Measuring the Economic Value of Employee Performance* by Jac Fitz-Enz. Designed to explain how to measure employee cost and productivity on multiple levels—organizational, functional and the management of human capital—much of this work is data-driven, but it, too, offers potent stories and case studies. Our favorite has to do with a story told by award-winning (including the Nobel and Albert Einstein) physicist Richard Feynman, who when he was part of the Manhattan Project was asked to take over a group from IBM, who had completed only three projects in nine months. Chosen by the Army from all over the country, their job was to "punch" numbers on IBM machines—with zero knowledge of what the numbers meant. Feynman wangled the security types to let him explain the mission. Here, in his words, is the joyous result of inclusion:

*"Complete transformation!
They began to invent ways of doing
it better. They improved the scheme.
They didn't need any supervising in the
night; they didn't need anything. They
understood everything: they invented
several of the programs that we used....
We did nine problems in three months,
which is nearly ten times as fast."*

Interestingly enough, the very act of measuring can activate disparate reactions, based on cultural backgrounds and experiences. In their book *The Spirit Level: Why Greater Equality Makes Societies Stronger*, authors Richard Wilkinson and Kate Pickett cite a Stanford study in which some students taking a college admissions test were told the results would include a measure of their ability and others were not. Among white students, it didn't matter. African-Americans, on the other hand, performed much more poorly when they thought they were to be evaluated.

The authors also cited research that revealed that members of ethnic minority groups have fewer health problems if they live in areas where there are others like themselves, as compared with their often more affluent counterparts who have "moved up" to mixed neighborhoods. Called the "group diversity effect," this was first discovered as related to mental illness, and then also proven true for heart disease.

We discussed several pages ago how insidious unconscious bias can be. Similarly, there are multiple instances of people whose intentions, to themselves and to some others, appear to be considered and kind—in other words, conscientiously inclusive. We offer for your examination in this arena two books: *The Leaders' Guide to Unconsciocus Bias: Reframe Bias, Cultivate Connection and Create High-Performing Teams* by Pamela Fuller and Mark Murphy with Annie Chow and *Nice Racism: How Progressive White People Perpetuate Racial Harm* by Robin DiAngelo.

Both books are rich with learning opportunities, but we are choosing to concentrate here on the subject of intentionality. In defining the different kinds of bias, for example, *The Leaders' Guide* names instances wherein we judge ourselves by our intentions and others by their results "attribution bias." In the chapter in her book titled "What's Wrong with Niceness?" DiAngelo includes in her list "helping others to maintain face and elevating intention over impact. As she explains further: "Niceness requires that racism only be acknowledged in acts that *intentionally* hurt or discriminate."

One of the core issues of effective inclusion, of course, is taking responsibility not only for actions, but failures to act. Books like these remind us to call those out.

Another differentiator in LATAM is
that the companies and job positions
are inherited. So, the entrepreneur
knows he is not getting anything from
someone and has to create out of
nothing, and with that, he is going to
look for an objective, and many times
he has to encounter failure many times.
It requires a lot of resiliencies. In our
countries, a lot we get is inherited.

~ Alejandro Valenzuela | CEO of Banco Azteca

CLOSING THOUGHTS

PEDRO DAVID ESPINOZA

It's always a special moment when you are at the end of writing a book. This was a crucial moment: a defining moment given that Jorge and I approached Maria as a co-author to add her invaluable insights and perspectives. While much has been done to improve inclusion, there is still much more to be achieved in the next five years. For example, there are still many Fortune 500 companies who lack a Hispanic board member, even though Hispanics account for nearly 20% of the US population. Numbers get worse when it comes to Hispanic representation in the senior leadership teams of Fortune 500 and S&P 500 companies.

I wanted to personally thank you, each one of you, our readers for being on this journey with us. Words are not enough to describe my gratitude towards my team (Maria and Jorge) on this outstanding adventure. From interviewing public leaders and Fortune 500 CEOs in Davos at the World Economic Forum, to meeting with Presidential Cabinet Members in Washington, it has been a joy to write this book. I've learned so much from spending countless hours through 1:1 meetings with top global leaders. Not only have I learned about inclusion and the future of work, but also about failing forward, grit, and tenacity.

Genuinely, I'd like to close this book by challenging you. Yes you! How are you paying it forward? You don't need a title to be a CEO. You don't need to be a billionaire to help another billionaire. You don't need a title to be a leader. I encourage you to ask yourself, who are you sponsoring? Who are you vouching for? Whose logo are you wearing on your t-shirt? If you want to see more females and people of color in leadership, inclusion starts with you (with I). I encourage you to start supporting someone in your workplace, business or environment. It all starts with you speaking highly of them, vouching for them, and endorsing them. Investing in each other makes the difference.

I cannot emphasize enough the importance of sponsorship. I would not be here, without the countless sponsors I've had as a startup founder, TED speaker, author, entrepreneur, and tech investor. To be candid, I don't reveal my age much; I'm 28. I'm grateful to say I've accomplished what I've accomplished thanks to the endorsements I've received. Thanks to the Fortune 500 CEOs, Fortune 500 Board Directors, University Presidents, Presidential Cabinet Members, State Governors, and Venture Capitalists who have endorsed me in front of others—especially in my absence in the boardroom, the hiring room, the promoting room. If I can do it, you can do it too. I came to this country ten years ago with zero network. I started a tech company at Stanford when I was 19, raised capital, wrote my first book with Jorge at the age of 24, gave a TED talk at the age of 23, and graduated from Berkeley Haas at the age of 22. A lot of it thanks to the people who were backing me.

Hence, to move the needle, one needs many sponsors. That is why today, I devote 100% of my team to preside and lead over Pan Peru USA. A social venture that empowers women to become entrepreneurs. Inclusion starts with I. We must be intentional. Could I start another startup? Yes. Another company? Yes. But I am intentional and passionate today, this year, to empower and equip more females in the most rural areas of Peru to become entrepreneurs through leadership development, microfinance, and support. I encourage you to start sponsoring others. A sponsor is invested, someone who pushes you. Someone who is not a mentor. Mentors give you advice. Sponsors are the ones who invest not only their financial capital but social capital in you.

It is no surprise that people of color are over-mentored yet under-sponsored...same with women. We need advocates in corporate America and globally to commit more support to each group. I encourage each of you to get involved and thank you in advance for fighting to improve everyone's work conditions. You see, I was inspired to write this book by my mom Julia who's an engineer and my sister Dr. Karina who's a medical doctor (physician), Stanford Class of 2012. I was always surrounded by powerful women; that was the norm for me in Peru. However, when I immigrated to the U.S. (Silicon Valley) as an 18-year-old student, I encountered a different culture; one where corporate America devalues a woman's contributions. Why are there more CEOs today named John than the total number of female CEOs? I expected more diverse representation in corporate America's leadership given the great strides toward equality in the United States, especially in one of the most innovative places on earth: San Francisco. There is something wrong, and we collectively need to fix it. We need more men to support their female colleagues. We need non-people of color to vouch for people of color. Most people who've helped me in my career, have been non-Hispanic. We all need each other. Let's do it! Let's go!

MARIA LENSING

The topic of Inclusion remains a controversial one. And that's unfortunate because it shouldn't be. There is no doubt of the value of diversity in every aspect of business, there is too much data available that proves that businesses that can harness the true power of diversity perform better than those that do not. The problem becomes when diversity is not understood as a business enabler and is instead viewed as a necessary evil.

Let's take an imaginary retail company as an example. If the leadership said, "we need to hire more women because it's the right thing to do," while the statement itself is not wrong, the connection between the action and the business result is not clear. This ambiguity leaves too much room for interpretation and since most of us interpret situations based on our experiences, unconscious biases will rear its ugly head. If instead the CEO would say, "we need to hire more women because not only are they 50% of the demographic we serve, but the data shows that 80% of the purchasing decisions in a household are driven by women. We would benefit from their perspective as we look at our plans for growth for the future." Do you have a harder time arguing with that? And, if a woman were to fail at a role, would this new positioning help us limit the failure to a mismatch of capabilities instead of a mismatch in concept (in other words, the person failed instead of women in general being a failure).

This is why the nuances of awareness, communication, and understanding of the current culture, are critical for all of you reading this book to understand and address. Diversity is important, but without an intentional effort to allow for inclusion the positive outcomes will not follow.

Change starts with one person. It starts with courage and vulnerability and allows for others to follow that example. To those that are skeptical of inclusion, please take this different approach and be data-driven in your position, think in terms of business outcomes, and I'm convinced you will see incredible results. And for those that are supportive of inclusion already, then it's time to act. If not now, then when? If not you, then who?

For those that know me, you know that I will always end with a call to action. My call to action for you is to internalize your true views of diversity and inclusion, allow yourself to vulnerably identify where you need to modify, and start working on being a champion of inclusion right now. It starts with understanding. It ends with the power to achieve more than you thought possible.

JORGE TITINGER

Coming to the end of a book is always bittersweet, while on the one hand, we want to have closure and declare completion; on the other hand, the journey was so enjoyable that we don't want it to end.

Part of what made this particular journey enjoyable for me was the addition of Maria as one of our co-authors. Pedro and I thought it important to add a female voice and viewpoint, and we were lucky to have Maria join us on this project. Her perspectives, viewpoints, and insights have definitely added to the value of this book and to the narrative that we present to our readers. Thank you, Maria!

As we mentioned at the beginning of the book, when we first set out to write *The Real ROI*, we intended to focus on highlighting how much progress had been made in the different areas of DEI since the publication of *Differences That Make a Difference*, and then the COVID pandemic hit. We are all aware of the massive financial and health chaos it produced around the world, but for me, one of the most dramatic impacts was the speed of change. It happened almost instantly. The world was thrown into a state of fear. When you combine fear with a lack of data and understanding, the result is not good. It suspends logical thinking, and it widens chasms.

The realm of DEI was no exception...to some extent it really tested the commitment of companies and other organizations to be more inclusive, and it separated those fully committed and those that were just checking the box. But the pandemic also brought a whole host of changes that needed to be addressed anew. It is these new changes and challenges that we hoped to bring forward in the book, and they make inclusion, true inclusion, an even bigger priority.

One of the biggest, and in my opinion, more permanent changes that the pandemic brought to us is the remote work or work-from-home (WFH) modality. At first, I, like many people I spoke with, thought this would last a few weeks to a few months; so, sending people to go work from home, with little or no anticipated planning was ok...(Kudos to those companies that had already developed protocols and practices for remote work.) But when it became clear this was here to stay, it challenged so many of our practices and behaviors that it necessitated a new lens through which to look. Our unconscious biases became harder to detect, our communication practices became challenged, our ideas on "whom" to include needed to change, the digital divide became more pronounced, trust amongst employees and employers was severely eroded, and of course, there was the Great Toilet Paper crisis of 2020.

I hope we have done a good job throughout the book of bringing attention to the different aspects that impact inclusion and thereby giving you a better viewpoint and some ideas for action.

It does not matter what your organization is all about, it doesn't matter if you are a startup, a multi-billion-dollar company, if you are restructuring, or simply growing—all of it gets done better when there is inclusion. And the results are often even more promising than expected.

Let's not forget that we need diversity because we have groups to include. And that inclusion is not a natural consequence of a diverse team or organization. We need to design for it. Inclusion is the achievement of a work environment in which all individuals are treated fairly and respectfully, have equal access to opportunities and resources, and can contribute fully to the success of the organization. And it is a two-way street: one should not be "waiting to be included," one should be proactive about it.

Absolutely critical for inclusion are communication and trust. Both elements are more challenging in the WFH world.

Communicating digitally is different from what most of us are used to. Gone are the physical clues that we have learned to read when we communicate in person, so we need to develop better digital body language. And trust...we really need to rebuild it. I really like Horsager's *The 8 Pillars of Trust*; are those present in our organizations? What can you do to build those pillars?

Progress has been made, but the game changed in 2020. The rules of the game, what's allowed, what's required, and what's forbidden are different in this post-pandemic world, so there is still more work to do. I thank our readers, because more than likely, you are all playing the game and are in it to succeed.

PERSPECTIVES ON POINT CONTRIBUTORS